PRAISE FOR
DISTRIBUTION LAND

"Finally we find simple and clear steps to organizing your financial affairs. *Distribution Land* provides the reader the tools to live life on purpose and be prepared financially. It was not raining when Noah built the ark. The actual client stories and the content of this book should motivate anyone reading it to understand why they need professional help and a written plan to have success in their financial affairs."

Michael Herman, ChFC
Golden Wealth Solutions, Inc

"In the U.S., those who reach 65 have an *average* life expectancy of another 18.8 years. In addition, one in 20 Baby Boomers will live to be age 100! Increasing longevity offers today's retirees opportunities that previous generations never experienced, but unprecedented challenges as well. 'Making the money last' is a complex issue, and pat answers and rules of thumb are wholly inadequate. In *Distribution Land*, Martin Higgins, CFP® does a masterful job off addressing the pitfalls that must be avoided as individuals transition from earning income to withdrawing income from savings and investments, and he makes a bullet-proof case for the importance of written retirement income plans that are customized based on each client's unique set of values, priorities, and life circumstances."

Carol Anderson
President, Money Quotient

"I'm very impressed by the author's insistence that we should find someone who emphasizes meeting with us as a couple, and listening to the fears and concerns that I have, in order to develop recommendations that will work for the both of us. I am confident that our advisor is managing our retirement investments with both of us in mind, just as he discusses in his book. If Dave were to pass away before me, my wishes and interests will be well-protected (with Wills, Trusts, and investments), and it is a tribute to our advisor that he has made sure that our value-based goals and plans are in place."

Stephanie Salewski

"Like many folks entering retirement, I felt comfortable with our family savings and investments. We didn't have a formal retirement 'plan', and I didn't think we needed one. But I knew I didn't have all the answers, so I set up an interview with a Retirement Income Planner to clarify my thinking and get some objective advice. What followed was one of the more humbling, yet truly fortunate, experiences in my life. He challenged my assumptions and inconsistencies in a blunt yet reassuring manner, and suggested real strategies to improve our retirement. We were drifting into *Distribution Land*, unaware of the many potential dangers to our retirement nest egg. It became clear that we did, in fact, need a retirement plan, with goals and objectives, based on our family values. He clearly wanted to understand our values, goals and objectives, and he invested a lot of time in learning about us, and what we thought about different issues. This has made all the difference. In his book, Marty Higgins emphasizes communication, sharing, and joint decision making, in order to establish a realistic plan. My wife and I couldn't agree more. We now have a friend who meets with us periodically, who is available to discuss a wide range of issues that may affect our retirement, and who manages our investment decisions. We have found a top-notch professional who has our back. I sleep very well at night."

Dave Salewski

"Preparing for, transitioning into, and travelling through retirement requires a long-term relationship with a knowledgeable advisor who becomes an integral part of your life planning, helping to set meaningful expectations and contingencies, put protections and contingencies in place, make necessary adjustments as events occur, and remain at your side as your future evolves. We are fortunate to have such guidance in place. Implementing this life plan has not only given us joint control of our finances, but peace of mind and confidence that we have the maximum potential for a secure future together. It is important that both spouses are completely involved in this planning process and execution; this is essential for success. We are making sound joint decisions, and we have the correct focus with no distractions. In addition, our ongoing financial and future activity discussions are open, constructive, and enjoyable. The transition into retirement should be set at a rate that is comfortable to both spouses. In our case, one spouse has continued to work part-time, reducing the work hours gradually as other desired activities have been discovered. *Distribution Land* details the essential retirement planning components that have worked exceptionally well for us."

Bill & Elaine Blakemore

"With more and more people approaching retirement it is more important now than ever that people realize Income distribution is much different than Income accumulation. With income accumulation we had time to recover from our mistakes in Income distribution mistakes can be ever so costly. This book is outstanding and gives great insights and stories to help people realize these dangers in this ever changing world of income distribution. It will be an invaluable resource to whoever reads it. Thank You Marty for taking your time and putting this in writing to help everyone."

Anthony G. Engrassia, ChFC, LUTCF
Financial Planner, Rocky Mount, NC

"For years the financial industry was talking about dollar cost averaging, a disciplined investment approach for the accumulation phase. Soon the industry may need to start talking about 'dollar loss averaging' as assets dwindle and markets gyrate. As we enter the Distribution Era and it will require more the same level of discipline. We are entering unchartered waters and fortunately Marty Higgins has done the work of a cartographer in *Distribution Land* that will enable you to both survive and thrive in the times ahead."

Mitch Anthony,
Author, The New RetireMentality

"As a relatively new retiree, *Distribution Land* has provided me with specific advice around financial planning as I crossed the bridge from Accumulation Land into retirement. The formal written financial planning process has helped to eliminate, for me, the fear of the unknown, and provided me with a sense of comfort, confidence, and stability".

Jack Morrison

"Kudos to Martin Higgins for creating a guidebook to help boomers navigate the largely unchartered territory of *Distribution Land*. A readable, fun and informative book."

Moshe A. Milevsky
The IFID Centre, York University, Toronto, CA

"Retirement is defined as a withdrawal from active service. But it does not mean a withdrawal from an active life! It means a chance to go places, do things, and enjoy life. It's a journey that could possibly last 30 years or more. But like any journey there are many dangers that if not identified can wreak havoc on what should be a happy time. Marty's book *Distribution Land* is the retirement traveler's guide to help you maximize your retirement year's opportunities and minimize the dangers that lie ahead. Use it as you would a trusty compass, map, or in today's world a GPS to have a happy and safe trip through retirement."

Danny Smith
President, Daniels Financial Group, Inc.

"My father worked tirelessly to provide financial opportunity for his family even when he wasn't going to be around to steer the ship anymore. His goals were clear: keep mom at her standard of living and leave a generous inheritance to his children. The underlying principles and planning processes discussed in *Distribution Land* have provided a roadmap to meet my father's goals for over 15 years. As a daughter helping her mom to keep her husband's ship on course, I encourage those in or near retirement to learn then practice the lessons of this book. As a woman, I urge you to start NOW. Until there is true wage parity and our earning power equals a man's, our only advantage is Father Time. You will be surprised, as I was, of the many opportunities and the sense of security in *Distribution Land* when a trusted advisor is part of your team."

Carol Schmidt

"This book is a must read for anyone within 10-years of retirement or less, or even recently retired. Retirement is not for the weak or faint of heart and Marty Higgins does a masterful job in providing insight and the tools needed to help retirees navigate through this strange new world of *Distribution Land*. I am a financial advisor and having been helping people take the confusion out of retirement for more than twenty-nine years and I found the content of this book invaluable, even at this stage of my career!"

Jay Van Beusekom RHU, LUTCF
President & CEO, Jay Van Beusekom Financial Advisor, LLC

DISTRIBUTIONLAND

DISTRIBUTIONLAND

A RETIREE'S
SURVIVAL MANUAL
for Transitioning to a World of
New Rules &
Unexpected Dangers

MARTIN V. HIGGINS, CFP®

Published by Advantage, Charleston, South Carolina.
Member of Advantage Media Group.

ADVANTAGE is a registered trademark and the Advantage colophon is a trademark of Advantage Media Group, Inc.

Printed in the United States of America.

ISBN: 978-1-59932-359-6
LCCN: 2014952507

Cover design by George Stevens.
Interior design by Kim Hall.

This publication is designed to provide accurate and authoritative information in regard to the subject matter covered. It is sold with the understanding that the publisher is not engaged in rendering legal, accounting, or other professional services. If legal advice or other expert assistance is required, the services of a competent professional person should be sought.

Advantage Media Group is proud to be a part of the Tree Neutral® program. Tree Neutral offsets the number of trees consumed in the production and printing of this book by taking proactive steps such as planting trees in direct proportion to the number of trees used to print books. To learn more about Tree Neutral, please visit www.treeneutral.com. To learn more about Advantage's commitment to being a responsible steward of the environment, please visit www.advantagefamily.com/green

Advantage Media Group is a publisher of business, self-improvement, and professional development books and online learning. We help entrepreneurs, business leaders, and professionals share their Stories, Passion, and Knowledge to help others Learn & Grow. Do you have a manuscript or book idea that you would like us to consider for publishing? Please visit advantagefamily.com or call 1.866.775.1696.

*To my loving wife Terri who
supports everything I do.*

*To my late dear friends, Ken Horowitz,
Jimmy Beal and Paul Bustard, who without
their support early in my career this book and
possibly my career may not have been possible.*

*And in loving memory of my parents,
Vince and Adele for instilling in me the
confidence and work ethic to succeed.*

{ ABOUT THE AUTHOR }

Martin V. Higgins is founder of Family Wealth Management, L.L.C., an independent wealth management firm. He specializes in providing tax-efficient strategies designed for preserving and growing family wealth.

 A Certified Financial Planner (CFP™), Higgins is past president of the South Jersey Chapter of the Society of Financial Service Professionals, and the Estate and Financial Planning Council of Southern New Jersey. He was also recognized by the Million Dollar Roundtable as a Top of the Table Producer, an award earned annually by fewer than one-tenth of 1 percent of the world's insurance producers. With five professional designations, Certified Financial Planner (CFP), Chartered Life Underwriter (CLU), Accredited Estate Planner (AEP), Registered Health Underwriter (RHU), and Life Underwriter Training Council Fellow (LUTCF), "I consider myself a student of the profession," Higgins says. "I have focused my entire career on education. I know a lot of people in different professions with 25 years of one year's experience—they're simply just repeating the same thing they started doing 25 years ago, over and over again. I don't believe that they're any smarter or adding any

more value than they were 25 years ago. The world is full of people like that."

As the president of Family Wealth Management and creator of "The WealthCare Process" (a program designed to simplify clients' financial affairs), Marty has shown a commitment to his own lifelong learning for the benefit of his clients, earning an impressive five industry professional designations to include the Certified Financial Planner (CFP) and Accredited Estate Planner (AEP). The past president of the Estate and Financial Planning Council of South New Jersey and the Society of Financial Services Professionals of Southern New Jersey, Marty also has been the recipient of many well-revered industry honors. He was a 2014 recipient of the Women's Choice Award for Financial Advisors and Firms,* a 2012 Senior Market Advisor of the Year finalist**, and a 2000 inductee into *Research Magazine's* Advisor Hall of Fame.*** Marty also has been featured in national magazines, including *Forbes* and *The National Underwriter.*

Higgins is co-author of and contributor to two books. *Dream, Inc.* features 32 Philadelphia-area entrepreneurs and how they built successful companies from scratch, and he also contributed to Dan Kennedy's book *The Ultimate Success Secret.* Higgins has been a featured speaker throughout the country and overseas, as well as for many company training programs. He regularly contributes to various industry magazines and local media.

"I altered the direction of my practice close to 15 years ago," he says. "I wanted to focus strictly on retirement income planning and to get ahead of the wave of boomers going through that phase.

"I actually went out and did my own research via a series of luncheons with families, couples, widows and others. "We did our own research, and crafted our own approach based on the type of experience and relationship people told us they wanted from a financial advisor."

The aim was to learn what people needed in a financial advisor relationship and what frustrations they had faced. "One interviewee that I met with told us of his experience with a previous firm. He and his wife were retiring and they decided that they needed a financial plan. They met with an advisor at a major firm, he designed a plan, transferred their money, and that was it—no follow-up. He said it was like he and his wife wanted to go on this fantastic journey and what they got was a boat and a map and were sent out to sea with a *bon voyage*—as if the only real plan was to get his money. The research came up with some dominant themes and created what we call the WealthCare Process. One core principle was that not only would we write these plans, but we would become stewards of the plans as well."

Higgins's many years of experience in the financial industry began after he was laid off from his construction job after high school. That was in 1972. "My family insurance agent asked if I wanted to come in for an interview—and by 1978 I had become a manager at the age of 24, and here I was telling men and women with families what to do." Soon he was engaged and buying a house, and decided to get life insurance for himself.

"Tough day?" a nurse asked during the exam. "They're all tough days," he told her. He was in management at the time and had grown weary with people's lack of work ethic. "Honey," she said, "you're 26 years old and your blood pressure is 158 over 120. You're about to blow out this window."

That was when he knew he had to do something different. "I talked to my fiancé, now my wife, and my dad, and said I was going to quit as a manager." That was October 1980, and he since has received the most consecutive Chairman's active Council awards in Mutual of Omaha's history.

Higgins earned his CFP designation in 1984, and has since earned four others within the industry. He is a Registered Representative of and offers securities through Mutual of Omaha Investor Services, Inc., a Registered Broker/Dealer, Member FINRA/SIPC. In addition to this, he is an Investment Advisor Representative and offers advisory services through Mutual of Omaha Investor Services, Inc., an SEC Registered Investment Advisory Firm. Insurance products and services are offered by various underwriting companies. Underwriting company is dependent upon insurance product sold. Family Wealth Management, LLC and Mutual of Omaha Investor Services, Inc. are not affiliated.

Higgins has lived in the South Jersey region all his life. He, his wife Terri, and their three children share a love of travel, local culture, and sports, including golf, baseball, lacrosse and hockey, as well as *all* of the Philly sports teams.

The Women's Choice Award Financial Advisor program was created by WomenCertified Inc. The Women's Choice Award Financial Program is based on 17 objective criteria associated with providing quality service to women clients such as credentials, experience and a favorable regulatory history, among other factors. Financial advisors do not pay a fee to be considered or placed on the final list of Women's Choice Award Financial Advisors, though they may have paid a basic program fee to cover the cost of comprehensive review and client survey. The inclusion of a financial advisor within the Women's Choice Award Financial Advisor network should not be construed as an endorsement of the financial advisor by WomenCertified or its partners and affiliates and is no guarantee as to the future investment success. Women's Choice Award* Financial Advisors represent less than 1% of financial advisors in the U.S. As of June 2014, of the 622 candidates considered for the Women's Choice Award, 104 were named Women's Choice Award Financial Advisors. This portion is updated monthly: please access updated monthly content at http://www.womenschoiceaward.com/financial-advisor-information/

**Nominees were evaluated by the editorial staff of Senior Market Advisor based on the following criteria. 1) Nominees had a minimum of five consecutive current years as an advisor 2) Have sold a minimum of $5 million in annuity/life insurance premium in PERSONAL production during 2011; or have sold a minimum of $400,000 in LTCI premium in PERSONAL production during 2011 3) Clear a 7-year background check for civil, criminal and business violations by the National Ethics Bureau (for complete details about the background check, visit http://www.ethics.net/) 4) Have an average client age of 60 or older 5) Be able to demonstrate a commitment to community involvement.

***2000 Research Magazine Hall of Fame candidates must pass our rigorous screens, including: service for a minimum of 20 years in the industry, substantial assets under management, superior client service, and recognition from their peers and the broader community for the honor they reflect on their profession.

{ ACKNOWLEDGMENT }

With this book, you are not alone.

My nearly one-year-old granddaughter (our first grandbaby, so far) is a prodigy. And wouldn't we all say the same of our kids or grandkids, given the opportunity to publish such news?

Ok, so "prodigy" may be a bit of an overstatement, but I can tell you this – that baby girl of ours is a pro at trusting those plump legs of hers to walk, run and even downright gallop. And she has been for some months now. My daughter is told regularly by strangers on the street that this walking-before-you're-one-year-old thing is quite extraordinary. We like to think it's only the beginning of greatness.

Just goes to show that we're all really good at something.

Having said that, though, here's what I'm not so good at. I'm not good at diagnosing the simplest health issues let alone the more complex ones that doctors see every day. I'm not good at debating in court someone's motivation for committing petty crime. I'm not someone who can paint the kind of art anyone pays to look at, I'm not a chef who can prepare decadent meals for hundreds of hungry patrons at once, and I'm not a PGA golfer (though I like to think I might be someday). For those of you who excel in these categories, I'd like to thank you for diagnosing, debating, painting, cooking and inspiring me to improve my golf game. I'm guessing, considering you have this book in hand, that you also are someone who has been good at accumulating money during your earning years. You and I have that in common.

After nearly 40 years of learning an industry that's ever-changing and complex, doctors, lawyers, artists, chefs, golfers, teachers, actors, event planners, CEOs, CFOs, brick layers and psychologists (to name but a few) move from earning a future to living one. Making the transition from accumulating money full time to distributing it full time requires the same type of expertise and education that any other field demands. If you proceed into distribution land alone, you may find that your tried-and-true practices of financial management (perfected during your 40-some years of accumulation) will actually work against you there. With this book, you are not alone.

Though the pages here do include a near-lifetime's worth of data and knowledge about financial planning in distribution land, you also will find here years' worth of stories that represent real people. I learned early on in my career that there is no such thing as a one-sized-fits-all approach when you're working with humans and their dreams. My clients have worked hard and planned well for years and they demand (and deserve) that planning to come to fruition now. Don't you deserve the same?

This book will give you the "legs" so you walk, run and gallop into distribution land with a toddler-like enthusiasm. I like to think it's only the beginning of your greatness.

{ FOREWORD }

Retirement for your parents was something that just happened, they really didn't have to plan for it. See, in the 1980's, you typically worked for the same company for thirty years. They then held a nice retirement party, presented you with a shiny gold watch and gave you a guaranteed paycheck for the rest of your life in the form a pension. Wow! You could take a cruise, join the country club and literally live Happily Every After!

Your retirement will likely not look like that. Pensions have disappeared for almost everyone other than government workers. The success of your retirement is not about the success of your former employer – it is really about how much money you were able to save and then, even more importantly, how do you turn that money into enough income to last you the rest of your life. If you take out too much, you will likely run out of money. If you don't take out enough, you will live a suboptimal retirement.

This is what Distribution Land is all about. For most retirees, Distribution Land is a foreign, scary place. It doesn't look like anything they have ever seen or experienced before. Oh sure, they have learned how to SAVE money, how to INVEST money, but they may not have learned how to DISTRIBUTE money! In fact, most retirees don't WANT to distribute money. They try to "not touch their principal" and "stay in control" of their money. All the while, they are setting themselves up for failure – either spending too much or too little.

With the concepts in this book as your guide, you will have your own "GPS" to show you exactly where you are, where you SHOULD be going, and the safest way to get there. He will show you where the unseen risks are and how to avoid them.

In my Public TV Special Don't Worry, Retire Happy – 7 steps to Retirement Security, I talk about how important it is to have a plan. People who plan for their retirement are more confident about their retirement, they are happier in retirement, and most importantly, they are more successful in retirement than those who don't have a plan.

I also talk about how important it is to use a trusted Financial Professional. Retirement is NOT a do it yourself project. Hey, if you have a cavity in your tooth, I'll bet you don't go into the garage, search for the correct size drill bit, hold up a mirror and try to drill the cavity out yourself! Well, retirement happens to be a lot more important and more complicated than drilling a cavity.

The retirement landscape is changing quickly, companies are adding new products, benefits and features every day. How can YOU keep up with all of this? You can't. You need a professional who does this every day. Look, I am considered a Retirement Income Expert by many and I use a Financial Professional. Why? Because even though I know what I need to do to retire optimally, I don't follow the day to day changes in product offerings. Besides, retirement is so important that I want a second set of eyes on my plan. I get busy and I need someone to remind me that it is time to review the plan as well. You should do the same.

So, what are some of the minefields in Distribution Land? The Stock market might crash right before or right after you retire. How would that affect your plan? Inflation could decimate the purchasing power of the income that you were able to generate with your savings. Can you live on 50% less income? That is what 4% inflation will do to your purchasing power over a 20 year period of time.

Or what about deflation and the threat of another great depression – what would THAT do to your plan. Some people think that because the market has averaged over 10% per year since 1926 that they can withdraw 10%, or 8% or 6%, well, surely 4% per year, right? NOPE. Those numbers will likely have you running out of money before you run out of breath.

What about the need for long term care? Long Term Care services are very expensive. What happens if YOU need some care? Is that in your plan. And what about the granddaddy of all retirement risks – LONGEVITY. What would happen to your plan if medical technology continues to develop cures and solutions for our medical problems. What if you live to age 100 or 110?

See Distribution Land can be a scary and dangerous place. Make no mistake, Millions, no, Tens of Millions of people will be ambushed by one or more of these risks. But not you! What Marty has done in this book is not only share the risks that are out there. He also shares very simple solutions. Ways that you can take risks off the table!

I give public seminars all across the country. I, too, am on a mission to help people avoid these risks. Many people think retirement is so complicated. I disagree. In fact, I believe the ULTIMATE SUCCESS of your retirement will depend on your answers to my next two questions. And, no, I'm not going to ask you how big your 401k is or how expensive of house do you live in.

See the success of your retirement is NOT about your assets! This is a paradigm shift. Your assets can be lost, they can be stolen, swindled, sued, divorced or decimated in a market crash! The ultimate success of your retirement will depend on your answers to these two questions:

1. How much Guaranteed Lifetime Income Do you have?

2. Have you taken the key Retirement Risks off the table?

That is it! See retirement is ALL about income, and I argue – Guaranteed Lifetime Income. You cannot spend your assets, you need income. By using the financial strategies Marty discusses, you can set up an optimal retirement plan – one where you will NEVER run out of money. A plan which helps you feel more confident about your financial future. One designed to help minimize key retirement risks and leave an inheritance for your loved ones when you die.

Both Marty and I were reluctant authors that realized how important it was for our simple message to be heard. After reading this book, you will understand why we are both so passionate about our message!

I have been training financial advisors for over 30 years and speaking about retirement to clients all around the world. I've written 3 books on retirement, *Paychecks and Playchecks: Retirement Solutions for Life*, *Retirement Income Masters: Secrets of the Pros*, and my new book releasing in late 2014, *Don't Worry, Retire Happy*. All of my books have the same common theme…Your retirement does NOT need to be complicated. Proper retirement planning can be based on math and science.

If you are looking for an enlightened perspective on retirement beyond the traditional sense, put aside some time immediately to read this future best seller. Once you understand how simple retirement is, you will have plenty of time to enjoy it with your grandchildren instead of sweating every time you open the business section of the paper.

Tom Hegna, Author and Economist
www.tomhegna.com

{ TABLE OF CONTENTS }

INTRODUCTION - A SWEET AND SCARY LAND......... 25

CHAPTER ONE - THE NEW YOU.............................. 41

CHAPTER TWO - WHERE DO WE GO FROM HERE?.. 51

CHAPTER THREE - FINDING SOMEONE TO TRUST.. 61

CHAPTER FOUR - SO MUCH AT STAKE 77

CHAPTER FIVE - MONEY BY THE BUCKETFUL 91

CHAPTER SIX - FACING DOWN THE ENEMY.......... 115

CHAPTER SEVEN - WORRIED SICK......................... 129

CHAPTER EIGHT - THE 401(K) FALLACY.................. 143

CHAPTER NINE - FOOTPRINTS FOR POSTERITY...... 155

CONCLUSION - SAFE TRAVELS 167

APPENDIX 171

INDEX.. 179

{ INTRODUCTION }

A sweet and scary land

'Hmmm," I said as I scanned the analysis. I shook my head, and then looked up at the doctor who was sitting in my office waiting for the prognosis. "I'd like you to come back tomorrow, and bring your wife."

"Is everything all right?" he asked.

"I just want to show you the results."

He was the first of two doctors who met with me that same week in 1999 for financial advice. It was the week I realized I needed to answer a calling. I wanted to help people to avoid screwing up their retirement.

I call this "The Tale of Two Doctors," but the fact that they were doctors wasn't all that significant—they could have been teachers, or brick layers. What is significant is how their stories illustrate the need to plan early and earnestly for your retirement years.

That first doctor had about $500,000, all in certificates of deposit. He was contributing the maximum amount permitted to his retirement plan, all in the CDs, and he planned to retire within five to seven years. He was about 60. We did a retirement income projection for him. He didn't want to have anything to do with equities or anything else other than bank deposits. I ran the analysis.

When he and his wife returned, I explained that the income projection showed that they would be out of money before he even reached age 80. It wasn't as if they were requiring some exorbitant income. And the problem wasn't market performance. The problem was that the return on his investments was barely enough, if that, to keep up with what would reasonably be expected to be the rate of inflation.

"You're going broke," I told him. "You're doing it safely, if that makes you feel any better, but you're going broke."

"What can I do?" he asked. I told him he could work longer, for one. Or he could take the money out of CDs. He didn't want to do either. He was hoping that interest rates would somehow return to the 1980 yields.

Later in the week, I went to see the second physician in his office. He had a similar set of facts—he was about 60, maxing out his retirement plan, and wanted to work five to seven more years. However, this doctor had about $5 million put away, ten times as much as the first doctor.

His investments were almost all in technology and health care stocks. His buddy, a doctor out on the West Coast, was managing both of their portfolios and was hot on tech. He'd pretty much stopped practicing medicine in pursuit of NASDAQ riches. Do you hear the sound of a bubble bursting?

"Let me ask you a question," I asked the doctor. "Do you think you have enough money to live the rest of your life comfortably?"

"Yeah . . . what do you think?" He had called me in for a second opinion, if you will.

"I think you do. So why, then, are you trying to turn $5 million into $25 million? Because if it goes down to a million, you're going back to work. You're not going to be able to retire."

A year or so later, I asked how his buddy had fared. He'd lost almost everything—he'd taken a 90 percent hit in technologies—and was back to practicing medicine.

Seven years later, I unexpectedly heard again from that first doctor. He asked me if I'd changed my opinion about his investments and what he needed to do. I told him once again that he was on the path to going broke. The man was shopping. He wanted to find an adviser who would tell him what he wanted to hear. He'll eventually find someone. There are plenty of so-called "advisors" willing to sell him something.

Fear was the risk factor for the first doctor I saw that week. For the second, it was greed. A financial advisor has to work with people at each extreme—and fear or greed are at the heart of most financial failures.

A WHOLE NEW LANDSCAPE

Managing risk is the most important aspect of good retirement planning, not pumping up your investment return. Meeting those doctors drove that point home for me—and I began focusing my career on helping people manage their risk as they are heading into retirement—or, as I call it, heading into Distribution Land. It's that new land that you enter as you prepare for retirement and begin taking out the money that you put into investments all those years.

Distribution Land is totally different than what you've experienced. To this point, you have been in Accumulation Land, where time has been your friend. You were likely advised to put money away consistently. You weren't too concerned about whether the market soared or sagged; if it went down, it meant you could buy a greater number of shares at a bargain price. You were not planning to pull out the money soon for income. Your objective was to gobble up shares, and you felt confident that, based upon its historical performance, the market seems to rebound over time.

You didn't focus on the daily price because you knew that wasn't the price you'd eventually get. The price in the paper that day was someone else's price. It was for the person that day who needed to sell.

Now you are crossing through the mist into a new world, Distribution Land. Everything looks different. Now you are withdrawing money for income, and time is no longer your friend. If the market drops while you are pulling from your portfolio for your income needs, you are in trouble. You are not buying any more shares at a bargain; rather, you are forced to sell at just the wrong time—and you don't have years stretching ahead of you for a recovery. What you did before doesn't work anymore. In this land, you need different weapons for survival.

Just as your life has likely been nothing like your parents', your retirement probably won't be either. It's no longer as simple as signing up for Social Security, collecting your pension, and settling back. You will probably be more active, live and work longer, and, for income, need to rely more on what you've saved. And that means ensuring that this income has the potential to last for your lifetime and to weather rising health care expenses, inflation, and market ups and downs.

DANGERS LURKING BEHIND THE BUSHES

"O brave new world," Shakespeare wrote. "How many goodly creatures are there here!" He was not referring to Distribution Land where, yes, the wonders of life are lush, but beasts lurk there that are less than goodly. They can be, in fact, quite vicious. One must be armed.

In a way, they are like Transformers. They look like one thing, and then suddenly they're something else. One of them is called "sequence of return risk," which we will be discussing. In short: At this stage of life, you may be buying the very same investment that you bought in your accumulation years that averaged 8 percent over time. Now, it still may average 8 percent over time—but if the bad years come early, the beast has pounced. You may go broke, or have to drastically reduce your standard of living. Or, if you are lucky, you might escape the bite entirely. But don't count on it.

Don't be surprised to see The Internal Revenue Service sneaking around in Distribution Land as well. He knows you've paid into a retirement plan all those years, and he's here for his cut of the taxes that he let you put off paying. You thought you'd be in a lower tax bracket in retirement? Surprise! What you were told may very well not be the case for you because now the taxman cometh and you may find yourself in a higher tax bracket than ever. How did *that* happen? That, too, we will be discussing.

The Transformers and other threats will come at you on the other side of the mist, you can be sure. But remember that fear itself is a huge threat and can lead you into financial ruin. It is possible to feel confident about your financial decisions in Distribution Land, and in this book I will show you how to equip yourself with the weaponry, strategies, and resources that are designed to help keep you away from harm.

But you need to start now, before it's too late. Days turn into weeks, weeks turn into months, and before you know it, it's the same old thing and you are well into retirement without having addressed a thing. Nothing's going to change if you don't get started. It's critical to have your retirement plan in place. Tomorrow isn't promised, and you don't want your loved ones to pay the consequences of your procrastination.

FINDING COMFORT AND CONFIDENCE

Imagine a couple who had hit the jackpot in a casino for nearly a million dollars. They didn't need any of that money and wanted to leave it to their children. The money was incorporated into their formal written financial plan, and they met with their advisor on a regular basis to review.

The husband developed Parkinson's disease and passed away unexpectedly. At the receiving line in front of his casket, his widow introduced their advisor to one of their daughters, who lived out of state. They had never met each other until then.

"This is my financial advisor," the widow told her, and upon hearing that, the daughter warned her that she should make no financial decisions for six months to a year.

"Oh, no, honey, your father and I have worked with this advisor for years. I know exactly what I'm doing."

Hopefully, that would feel reassuring to the widow and to the daughter. It's often the case with older couples that the husband has taken care of all the finances and the wife knows little about them. When the husband dies, the widow's grief is compounded by money worries. Having a formal, written financial plan in place can help avert that. It helps to eliminate the fear of the unknown and also helps to provide increased levels of comfort, confidence, and stability.

Research shows that most widows change financial advisors within a year or so after their husband dies. (Investment News, January 1, 2012.) In my opinion, most advisors focus on the man. They figure that among people that age, the man will be the decision maker, so they don't ask the wife how she feels about anything. The advisor might not even know her—and when the man dies, she has no allegiance to that relationship.

A man called our office once to say he was coming in for advice and wasn't bringing his wife. I told him we'd have to wait until he could bring her—we don't want to work with just half of a couple. He explained, however, that this was a second marriage and they had carefully kept their financial lives separate. And that's fine. But had he said he didn't need her there because he handles it all himself, I surely would have reiterated to him that we only work with married couples if they come together—no exceptions.

You need a financial plan in place while you are alive and for the sake of your loved ones when you are gone. It eliminates guessing.

It is indeed the fear of the unknown that can hamstring you in retirement. Whether it's founded or unfounded, it comes down to uncertainty. Without a financial plan, you don't know whether you could fend off a real threat, and you may imagine a threat that doesn't exist, yet spend years scrimping. You deserve to enjoy life.

Imagine if you will, a couple in their 70s, in the early stages of their financial planning, and the wife is upset. She wants to go on vacation every year, but her husband insists they don't have the money. She wants a professional to weigh in.

It would make sense to prepare a cash flow analysis and income projection and talk to them about how much they thought such vacations would cost. The answer may be right there in black and white. Perhaps there is no reason why they shouldn't be taking yearly vacations.

And that's the real purpose of a financial plan. People feel frozen when they don't know what the future looks like. A couple may feel they need to hoard their money and not enjoy it, or at least one of the spouses feels that way. Next thing you know, one of them is too sick to go anywhere and they haven't done anything. It's a pleasure to be able to demonstrate to clients that they should be all right, that they can go out and enjoy the fruits of their labor.

"Do you have a written plan forecasting income and expenses in retirement, designed to analyze whether or not you may run out of money?"

YOU NEED A GUIDE

It's quite possible, in other words, that once you get into Distribution Land, with all your weapons arrayed, you will get out your binoculars and scan the horizon and see no threats—north, south, east, or west. What will you do? Hunker down in a cave anyway? Or will you go out to stroll on the veldt? If you have a plan in place, the more likely you will be to keep the beasts at bay—or just lying deep in the grass.

When you are heading into risky territory, you may need a guide. You can get on a raft and head down the Colorado River all by yourself for free, whether you know what you are doing or not. But with a guide by your side, you are far less likely to end up pounded by the white water. Most would choose to pay extra for the guide. In Distribution Land, it may be beneficial to partner with a retirement income specialist who can explain and guide you through the specific financial situations of concern to you—someone well versed in issues of retirement income planning, someone with experience who has been down the river before.

Our clients are typically pre-retirees and retirees, financially independent women, or successful entrepreneurs. To learn whether you will be a good match, we look at some key points. This is what we want to see:

- ◆ You are open-minded and have distinct goals.

- ◆ You are committed to developing and implementing a written financial plan.

- ◆ You should understand financial strategies and products.

- ◆ You understand the value of advice and want to delegate financial decisions and investment management to a team of competent professionals.

- ◆ You have realistic expectations.

- You have investable assets of a quarter million dollars or more.

- You are willing to refer us.

We call our relationship with clients "The WealthCare Process," and the first step is a discussion on whether we are the right fit for each other. Do you like us? Do we like you? Is what we offer a match with what you want? We will both have to enjoy working together.

FOCUSING ON GOALS

We focus on your goals. You need to know what you want to do in retirement so you can figure out whether you'll have enough income to accomplish it. You can't plan the trip until you know where you are heading, and you would be well served to have a map.

For every degree a plane flies off course, it will miss the target by 92 feet for every mile. After traveling 53 miles, the plane will be about a mile off course. Over time, the gap will increase. On a flight from New York City to Los Angeles, the plane would be over 40 miles off course.

Fortunately, airplanes have computer systems on board that help the pilot to make corrections in the course. The pilot has learned how to steer the plane back in the right direction when he has strayed from the route.

The pilot knows the starting point, the goal, and the flight plan. By reading his instrument panel, he knows when he gets off course and he knows what to do to get back on the path. His chief goal is to get to his destination safely.

A good retirement income planner will act as your pilot, navigating you so that you stay on course to your destination.

The goal for investing is not wealth in and of itself. It needs to have a purpose. There's no honor in being the richest person in the cemetery. The objective is not to beat the S&P 500. If the S&P 500 plunges 37 percent in one year, as it did recently, and your portfolio is down just 25 percent, should you expect to give a high five to your advisor? Perhaps an "attaboy?"

Think of it this way: If you are sitting at a blackjack table in Vegas with a pile of money that you have amassed, why would you put it all down on one more hand? At some point, enough is enough, and it's time to get out on the town. In other words, it's time to put the money to work and pursue your goals.

The objective is to make your goals attainable. We make sure that we're reaching toward what you want to do, whether that's to leave a large legacy to heirs, or to spend your last dollar as you take your last breath. Everybody's different, and we customize a plan that is unique to you. It's an art form, really.

Not only do we write the financial plan, but we are stewards of the plan. One of the advantages of working with a financial advisor is to keep you from making emotional decisions. When you get scared and want to make a bad decision, I'm there to grab your hand, talk you off the ledge, and tell you, "I've got your back." What kills a strategy isn't the investment or a lack of performance so much as it is the investor's behavior. You need someone to talk to.

"PEOPLE BEFORE NUMBERS"

I manage our relationship and your expectations, and then we outsource to unique ability. For the money management part, that would entail using professional money managers, people who do that full time for a living. Most advisors try to manage the money while also managing the people. I say pick one, because you can only do one well. Our focus is on the relationship and "understanding people before numbers"—which is the tagline of our practice. That is much of what makes us different.

And as I get to know you, I will understand how to help you manage the risks that you will face—or already are facing—out there in Distribution Land. Managing risk is the priority, and as you turn these pages you will learn more about the nature of those risks. I will identify them, chapter by chapter, and give you advice on how to deal with them effectively. I will show you strategies designed to help you fend off the threats so that you may be able to breathe free.

I will address what is probably your top concern as a retiree, a concern shared with most others your age: Will you have enough money to last the rest of your life? There's no reason to be unclear about that.

I will offer advice on how to find a good advisor and the importance of teamwork. I will help you sort through your concerns about taxes and fees, inflation, and other things to watch out for in this new land. A major one is your health. What if you or your spouse gets sick? Is there anything you can do to stop your life's savings from draining away?

What is your plan for long-term care? I didn't ask if you had long-term care insurance. I asked if you had a plan. Most people do not. They let whatever happens happen, and then they complain that they never saw it coming.

SLIPPING SAFELY THROUGH THE MIST

I will show you, in short, strategies designed to help you safely slip through the mist and enjoy your journey in Distribution Land. I will show you how to make the natural adjustment from those years in which your emphasis was on accumulating money to this new stage when your emphasis must be on preserving and distributing your money.

Truly there are beautiful things to behold in Distribution Land. You deserve to enjoy the scenery. "You can work for your money," I remember my father telling me, "or your money can work for you." You spent decades earning your pay, and now your savings may provide that income—if you set up your finances properly. You have to do it right.

Imagine yourself traveling upriver in a boat with your spouse, far from shore, and up ahead you see a lovely island. Let's call it the Island of Financial Security. You are trying so hard to get there, but you only have a one-horsepower motor—and the river current is three miles per hour. You see the island slipping further away as the current pulls you downstream. And if you encounter a headwind, all the worse.

Now, imagine yourself with a CD that pays 1 percent a year. But coming at you is an inflation rate of 3 percent a year. You get the picture: If that is how you are invested, financial security slips further away. And that's not even considering taxes, health care costs and whatever else you encounter—and you surely will. You are never going to make it to the island. What you have to worry about is the waterfall behind you.

Let me show you, in the chapters ahead, what to beware in Distribution Land, and some strategies designed to help you navigate your financial journey. These should be the best years of your life, but you can't wander around in this land like a zombie thinking that you will be just fine so long as you preserve the principal of your nest egg. You have many other issues to deal with: inflation, health care, taxes, fees, and the myriad emergencies that could befall you or your loved ones. Will you live longer than your money will last?

WHAT YOU DON'T SEE CAN KILL YOU

An accountant and his wife recently came to my office to prepare for their retirement in a few years. They had about $2.5 million in CDs and bonds, and they had figured out how much they wanted in retirement income. They presumed all was well. But my projection showed their portfolio in a death spiral by their early 80s.

"You know what that means, right?" I asked them. They risked running out of money.

"Yeah, it means I don't believe it, how's that?" the accountant said. I showed him the numbers, and as a CPA he understood them, of course—yet couldn't quite grasp why this would be happening.

"Have you ever seen *Jurassic Park*?" I asked him.

"Sure. Dinosaurs gone bad."

"Right. Remember the scene where the boy tells the archaeologist he wouldn't be afraid of a raptor?" I asked. "The guy shows the kid a petrified claw and demonstrates how a raptor could shred him to pieces. But then he explains that the raptor that would be staring him down wouldn't be the one he'd have to worry about. In fact, he wouldn't have to worry about him at all. See, the Velociraptors hunt in packs and it's the ones to the sides that are going to kill you, and you're never going to see them coming."

The CPA furrowed his brow.

"You were scared," I explained, "because you saw that market risk in front of you, staring you down. So you put all your money into CDs and bonds so you wouldn't have to worry about market risk. But off to the side—and I don't think you see it coming—are inflation and longevity as well as other risks that may kill you."

Dinosaurs don't roam Distribution Land, but you will face other perils. Don't be afraid. Be prepared.

{ CHAPTER ONE }

The New You

J erry seemed so eager to retire. "I started this 35 years ago, thinking I'd be there six months," he said. "And I've hated every minute." He stuck with it, for sure, yet it saddened me that he hadn't enjoyed his work.

They moved to Florida. Later, in retirement, he came in for a visit. "If I knew this was what it was going to be like, I'd have never retired. I hate every minute. I hate it in Florida."

So many people pull up their roots in retirement and leave their whole social circle. They start anew, far from home. No longer are they near friends and family. No longer do they see their acquaintances at work. If their career has ended, they may feel they have lost a sense of purpose.

Jerry was unhappier than ever. He thought retirement was going to mean his freedom. What it meant was that he abandoned the little bit of stability he had. And he didn't have enough money to take his boat out fishing—and that's his main hobby.

He had a pension and a decent amount of money, but he and Jean felt strapped because they hadn't anticipated spending $1,000 a month in tuition bills to help their daughter. Jerry's strategy was to spend as little as possible and let the savings grow and also delay his Social Security so that they would have more later—or rather, so that Jean would have more later. He wanted to make sure Jean would be all right without him. He figured he'd probably die soon; living this way was going to kill him.

"Look," I told him, "right now you're miserable. You're making everybody around you miserable. You're probably shortening their life expectancy. So what's the purpose of your strategy? To save for death? Why don't we open up the spigot so you can start taking out some money and start enjoying yourself?"

"Well," he said, "that's going to mean less for later."

"There might not be a later for you, the way you're going."

Fear holds so many people back. Some even hoard, fretting unnecessarily, while others seem oblivious about very real dangers they are facing. It goes both ways. The point is that you need help. You need to be able to get a grip on what your financial state truly is as you head into retirement.

Americans are retiring by the millions, and many others are coming to see that it's crucial to carefully plan for retirement. They understand that they may need a professional advisor.

A WHOLE NEW GAME

The shift toward planning for a retirement income is highly challenging. It's a new game at this time of life. The emphasis turns to risk management, which is much more complicated.

In many financial advisors' offices, the retirement planning process begins with a discussion about investments. However, before considering specific strategies or investment products, you must establish what it is you want to achieve. That's the beginning of real financial planning.

Financial goals often include an income that you can't outlive. You may want to help with the education of your grandchildren. You may want to leave a significant legacy to the people you love and must leave behind one day. These things can, and must, be the focus of planning and investing. To beat an index is not a real goal. Neither is doing better than another investor, or some benchmark, or the market. A goal is an aim for your life.

Some people enter retirement with visions of what it will be like that aren't quite what most people experience. Perhaps they have some idyllic image of sitting on the porch with the grandchildren bounding about. They may think of it as a string of vacations and cruises and living leisurely.

In truth, they may find that they can't imagine how they ever had time for a job because they're busy with so many things. Some may find they can't balance the budget and may have to go back to work.

Years ago, when my mother and father retired, I called one morning to invite them for a visit. "We can't," answered my mother. "We're so busy." "But you're retired," I pointed out, and she told me she hadn't realized she'd have so many things that would fill up her day. In retirement, people tend to have no trouble finding things to do. They stay active.

And they spend money. Saturday is the biggest spending day, when many people are off work. When you are retired, every day is like a Saturday. You look for things to do. You have to manage your cash flow—and that cash flow may well need to be sufficient to support at least one of you for three decades.

The core of our client relationships is cash flow management. Prospective retirees, when asked about their big plans, say "travel," almost with a common voice. It costs money to travel, you may have noticed. It costs something to visit the grandkids, unless they live nearby. Retirees need a clear idea about whether they have the resources to support that lifestyle they envision. Often, they find out that they have more than enough. But this is no time to guess. You have to know.

A FEAR OF LIVING TOO LONG

In the next several years, baby boomers will be retiring in droves, with fewer and fewer workers to support them in the Social Security system. The government's spending for Social Security will rise faster than tax income because the population over age 65 is growing faster than the working age population based on 2007 Social Security Annual Reports[1].

The country faces not only a tide of baby boomers but also an increase in life expectancy. In 1935, when Social Security began, retirement lasted but a few years. Today it lasts a few decades and longer. For a couple both aged 65 today, according to projections, there's a 50 percent chance that one will live to 92 and a 25 percent chance one will live to 97. The population is aging[2].

---

[1] Social Security - ssa.gov/history/pdf/tr07summary.pdf

[2] American Council of Life Insurers - acli.com/Tools/IndustryFacts/LifeInsurersFactBook/ Documents/FB11Mortality.pdf (11/18/2011)

When I explain to people that they need to plan for a retirement that may last two or three decades, they often seem incredulous. I say, "Let's play a little game." I ask them to read the obituaries over the next two weeks until we meet again and count up how many people died in their 90s. It's an eye opener. That settles the matter.

"I could design a financial plan for you," I tell them, "based on having enough money until age 82. But what happens if you are still living then?" You can buy life insurance to protect yourself against not living long enough. But protecting yourself against living too long is another matter entirely. In my opinion, many people have a primal fear of dying. These days, from a financial standpoint, their primal fear often is not that they will die too soon, but rather that they will live too long.

Many people hope to retire early and will be living longer—and that puts unprecedented demands on their nest egg. Talk to any stockbroker, and you will conclude that it seems like Wall Street's only solution is to buy more equities. But in my opinion, an investment strategy isn't a solution to a risk management problem. It simply adds another risk.

This new phase of life called retirement most certainly can be a troubling one. You have spent years in what I call Accumulation Land, and now you have to shift your retirement savings into Distribution Land. Most people don't even know there's a difference.

It's not all about the money. As we saw with Jerry, who hated his new life in Florida, it's also about the other huge changes that retirees face—the loss of a social circle, the loss of one's work identity. But money, and worrying about how to handle it, plays a major role.

MANAGING YOUR "PILE"

All of your career, you have been used to a paycheck coming in, and now in retirement that paycheck is gone. You have to create your own paycheck from your own resources, and that can feel quite unsettling. Social Security is uncertain and may be insufficient, and the days of private company pensions are nearly gone—replaced, for many people, by tax-deferred retirement plans, 401(k)s. Upon retirement, some fortunate people find themselves with a pile of money to manage somehow.

"What do you want?" I sometimes ask clients when they tell me it's their last day of work. "Shall we dump your pile in your living room to look at every day, or do you want to get a check in the mailbox each and every month?" In previous generations, people wanted checks. Now they think they have to maintain this pile and can't turn any of it into a check in the mailbox.

Let's suppose that a man is retiring from one of the major phone companies and visits with an advisor who all of his previous coworkers have used. He has been given the option of a pension or a lump sum. The pension looks rather attractive to him; however, all of his previous coworkers took the lump sum, so he's confused. He meets with the advisor, who recommends that he should take the lump sum.

"Why do you think that would be?"

Considering what has happened in the markets over the last decade or so, it is important to obtain a fair comparison of both options in order to make an intelligent decision.

For every case like that, there are others in which the lump sum might indeed make sense because the pension being offered isn't a great deal. The lump sum, if invested prudently, could serve better. It depends on the specifics of the situation.

In this post-pension era, you have to create your own cash flow. You have to take that pile and make it last for the rest of your life. You need to create that income stream in a way so that you feel more confident about your financial situation, and you won't be staring at the ceiling at night.

Your concerns in Distribution Land are certainly different than they once were. Once, back in your 30s and 40s, if you are like so many others, you were starting a family, buying a house, raising children, saving for college, paying off tuition—and increasing your debt load. You were advancing in your career and getting those raises and striving to accumulate money for the obligations ahead.

TIME IS NO LONGER ON YOUR SIDE

When you were younger, your biggest asset was time. You could afford more aggressive investments and more risks. You could count on having enough time to outwait the changes in the market. In fact, the volatility of the market could serve you well. You could buy equities inexpensively when the market was down and watch them rise to new heights in the boom years. You could invest consistently and continually, with optimism that over the years your investments would prevail. That's the principle of "dollarcost averaging," which we will discuss in Chapter 4.

Now, as you face years of retirement, your worries are different. Will you get smacked by the stock market just when you need your money for income? Will you run out of money? Will you pay too much in taxes every year? Will the government get the lion's share of your estate? Will you be able to help your children and grandchildren and other loved ones? Will you or your spouse become ill and need long-term care? Will inflation eat away at your savings? If you face an emergency, will you have enough cash on hand to deal with it? Those are common questions on fundamental issues that virtually all retirees face. These are universal concerns for people at this stage of life.

Here in Distribution Land, time is no longer is your friend. You don't have a long lifetime stretching out before you as you did in your 20s and 30s. The financial strategies that you once used may be counterproductive now. They can expose you to risk that you can't tolerate.

And you face another huge risk: inflation. If your investments don't keep pace with it or exceed it, inflation will insidiously eat away at your nest egg. All those years when you were earning a wage, you may not have paid much attention to inflation. You probably got regular raises, and you may not have suffered a reduction in purchasing power. But now, in retirement, you have to tame inflation yourself.

Let me repeat: Be prepared. If you don't plan properly, any number of situations can affect your retirement plan. Illness or incapacitation.

A stock market crash. An emergency. Your spouse dies, or divorces you. One or more of your children move out, multiply, and then move back home with you. Those are a few.

DON'T FUMBLE AT THE GOAL LINE

"It's really a shame," one man told me as I researched the real issues that retirees face. "My wife and I saved all this money. We were very prudent. We didn't accumulate a lot of money, but we had maybe a half a million dollars that we had put aside. Then my wife gets sick and she goes into a nursing home and she takes, like, $400,000 of it. It's kind of like I fumbled at the goal line of life." He said they hadn't planned for that. "We had no idea."

What others don't plan for is a stock market crash. Many learned that hard lesson just a few years ago. It's not unusual for otherwise conservative investors to see an upswing and try to get in on the action, but they're late to the party and the lights go out.

What about the retired couple who get a phone call one day from their daughter—her husband has left me, she cries, and may I come home with the kids and the dog? All of a sudden they're buying food for six instead of two, and replacing the carpet. Or maybe it's you who are getting the divorce; the rate among people in their 70s is higher than ever[3]. It doesn't take much imagination to see what that does to a retirement plan.

Or your spouse dies, and the survivor benefits just aren't what you thought they would be. Somehow you need to come up with an income that will get you through. A young widow, too, could

[3]Age Power by Ken Dychwald (2000)

face this situation. Suddenly, at the age of 30 or 40, long before she expected it, she finds herself needing to devise an income stream. If the wealth isn't sufficient, it's back to the workforce.

Life situations, in other words, have the power to propel you prematurely into Distribution Land, or send you packing back to Accumulation Land. But most all of those situations can be anticipated. You may be able to head them off at the pass.

Retirees need specific advice on longevity planning, managing withdrawals from retirement funds, transferring wealth to heirs, and many other complex issues besides how to allocate their assets. Too often, the focus is on the money and not the humanity.

You need a financial advisor who cares about you and thinks of you as a human being—not as a sheet of figures. You need to be clear about who the client is—you or your statements.

{ CHAPTER TWO }

Where Do We Go from Here?

Alice: *Would you tell me, please, which way I ought to go from here?*
Cheshire Cat: *That depends a good deal on where you want to get to.*
Alice: *I don't much care where.*
Cheshire Cat: *Then it doesn't much matter which way you go.*

—from *Alice in Wonderland* by Lewis Carroll

T he man began to weep.

He and his wife had come in for advice on handling their finances, soon after I changed the focus of my practice to retirement income planning. I began asking questions to get to the heart of what money meant to them. How did they want to be remembered after they were gone? What did they wish for their children and grandchildren?

And that's when the gentleman broke down. I could see how deeply important these matters were to him. He didn't seem upset or conflicted. He just seemed to profoundly appreciate being asked. I felt uncomfortable at first; I'm not out to make people cry, but I do want to reach the heart. I want them to know I care about them as human beings and not as purveyors of financial statements.

Money is one of the most stressful topics in a marriage, and emotions often surface when a couple comes in to my office to discuss how to handle finances. I've heard harsh words, and I've seen many tears. Family issues come to the fore. I hear disputes about children and stepchildren and who should get what. Often it seems as if they have never really talked about these things before. I've felt at times like a marriage counselor as raw feelings pour out in front of me.

IDENTIFYING PRIORITIES

If a couple haven't thought about these matters, it's high time they did. I strive to understand my clients, and I must know them well—their priorities and goals—before I can help them craft a financial plan for retirement. We don't just help them manage money. We help them identify how they feel about money and what they believe it should accomplish.

To understand people, I must examine their past, present and future. I need to look at the roots of their relationship with money. What were their first experiences with it? What was it like in the household where they grew up? That helps me know what motivates their decisions—and, in the end, they own their decisions. Often, clients ask me what I would do in a particular situation. But what I would do might not be best for them, and my job is to guide them toward the latter.

I need to hear from both husband and wife. I give them rules of engagement: While one is talking, the other must be quiet. The reason for that, in my experience, is there's usually one dominant spouse who likes to take charge of everything, and I must ensure a comfortable environment free of interruption.

As I talked with one couple, the husband told me about his dream of cruising around the Keys in a sailboat and visiting the islands. "I'm not doing that," his wife said. "I get seasick. No way." Wouldn't you think they would have already talked about that? But it's not unusual for one spouse to look at the other and say, "I never knew you thought that."

"MONEY IN THE CONTEXT OF LIFE"

A good advisor will have such discussions with clients. They should talk about the meaning of money and their goals and dreams. They need to share such things before the talk turns to finances, or I can't truly know how to help them. This is their life, their money, and their dreams.

Unfortunately, some advisors don't try to understand their clients that way. If the first thing an advisor does is ask to look at your statements, says Mitch Anthony, author of *The New Retirementality*, you should head for the door.

At times, I feel like a social worker, or a personal counselor, as well as a financial advisor. That's because everything that happens in people's lives affects their finances. We use a program called Money Quotient that helps us get to people's core values and beliefs and hopes for accomplishment. "Putting money in the context of life™" is Money Quotient's motto.

What I do is called Financial Life Planning. The orientation is toward goals.

"So what's your performance against the S&P?" a woman asked me once on her first visit to my office.

"Why does it matter?" I asked.

She seemed dumbfounded. "Well, isn't that supposed to be how I judge you?"

"Really? If we aren't addressing your financial goals, I don't think you'd be giving me an *attaboy* for doing a little better than the S&P in 2008, would you?" That's the benchmark that has been ingrained in investors for years because it's on many statements and performance reports, and it's not a successful strategy. The benchmark should be determined by your goals.

We help with planning your immediate, short range, and long-term goals. We calculate how much those goals would cost, and we try to build an income plan that is designed to accommodate them. We're not out to top the S&P 500. That's not what a goal is. We don't care about that any more than we care about your neighbor's tax return. Leave that for the cocktail party talk

We ask what you want in life. What's important to you? If it's a vacation each year with the kids and grandkids, we build that into your plan. If it's an education scholarship to your alma mater, we set that aside. Whatever you wish to achieve, we calculate it into the target rate of return that would be needed to fulfill it. We won't go after a 40 percent return just to beat some benchmark. We don't want to see you lose 40 percent.

When people don't have a focus, they can wind up competing against financial benchmarks. But when they have a clear vision of their retirement goals, they can start planning to reach those goals instead. That's why it's important to start the planning at least five years before retirement, so we can lay the groundwork and begin building.

YOU NEED A GAME PLAN

You can't just wing it. The Philadelphia Eagles are the big football team in my parts. You can be sure they have had extensive talks on strategy. The present coach, Chip Kelly, doesn't come out on Sunday morning after the national anthem and ask, "Okay, guys, anyone have an idea what we should do today?" They have a game plan. They've spent a week reviewing it. They can adjust it at halftime, but the strategy is in place. They don't make it up as they go.

But that's how a lot of people approach retirement. They wait until they're into it before they start planning. As a result, things may not work out as well as they would if they had addressed them earlier, and they can end up unhappy and disillusioned. They had grown weary of the daily race of their workaday life, but they may find retirement filled with new anxieties. They can't seem to slow down.

In retirement, you may well have every intention of keeping busy. You may have plans aplenty to keep you occupied, but at this point you should be able to decide where and when you do your running. By deciding your destination up front, you can set your own pace. You will know how much income you need to accomplish your goals and still live comfortably the rest of your days.

The "Retirement Red Zone," as Prudential calls it, should begin five years prior, and probably ten years if you are a business owner. Many people have an investment plan but no overall financial plan. Clear direction sometimes is totally lacking. People are so busy living and stomping out fires that they have never really stepped back to take a long view of what they want to do in retirement. They lack focus and priorities.

In their book *Comfort Zones*, Elwood Chapman and Marion Haynes put it this way: "Many people are so occupied with getting out of a career trap that they seem to care little about what happens after they leave their jobs. Too many people retire to nothing and then wonder why they feel empty and disenchanted."

If you suspect that describes you, we can do much to help you there. We can help you visualize the lifestyle that you will find most satisfying and fulfilling. Part of the Money Quotient program that we use is called "Retirement: Thinking It Through." We put our clients through some exercises, and their responses speak volumes about how they are viewing the years ahead.

As our clients approach retirement, we begin such conversations regularly, working with them as a team to help them envision and articulate their unique take on retirement. We suggest that they think of their goals as targets. They're something to aim for. They give life direction. By setting goals, they anticipate, plan and prepare. They focus on expectations.

Once they have articulated their needs and goals, we can look at costs. How much will that hobby pull from their savings now, and in the future? What will be the effect of buying a new car every five years? Of a vacation twice a year? Do they expect to remodel the kitchen soon, or ever? Will the house need a new roof? It's important to write these things down. That way, you won't be sidetracked by somebody else's agenda.

A major consideration is this: Do you want to enhance your own lifestyle as much as possible, or do you want to leave as much as you can to your children? That's going to have a big influence on the type of investments you make now. An advisor who specializes in such questions at this phase of life can help you sort through your options. You need to talk with someone who knows what you are dealing with in Distribution Land. You may feel a course of action is impossible, but the right advisor will help you create a plan that can work for you.

DON'T CHASE IMPOSSIBLE DREAMS

After we have identified the client's desires for retirement, it's time to take a look at the financial statements. That's when we find out whether the expressed goals are realistic.

One couple came to my office saying they wanted to retire in about five years, at age 60, and they wanted to pay for the kids' college educations, and they wanted to pay for two daughters' weddings. "Those are noble goals," I told them, and I figured they must have the assets to handle them. But all they had was $50,000 in an IRA.

I gave them the bad news: They would need to keep working, and they couldn't afford those tuitions and weddings. It was impossible for me to help them. When people hear that, they sometimes search for somebody who tells them otherwise and will validate their opinion. And they enter dangerous territory. Never forget: Fearsome creatures can get you in Distribution Land.

If you want help, you need to be willing to take advice—not blindly, of course, but once you develop a relationship of trust, you can delegate responsibility to someone knowledgeable in an area that is not your forte. Why else would you be seeking out an advisor? So you can talk about how smart you are? When prospective clients come to see us, we make it clear that we may not be a fit for them. Even if they choose us, we may not choose them.

Some people have the attitude that most advisors would shine their shoes just to get their business. We're in the business of helping people thrive in retirement, not patting their backs as they head into peril. That's why we place so much emphasis on defining goals and organizing life priorities; that's the only way we can discern the best way for you to organize your finances.

GETTING ORGANIZED

At this point, organizing the paperwork itself is an important step. Where are your documents? People sometimes don't even know, or they have only a vague idea. They're not even sure of the scope of their assets. Anyone who has ever administered an estate could attest to that. One of my clients, an accountant, came in one day looking flustered. One of his own clients had just dumped another box of paperwork on his desk—newly discovered documents from an estate he was trying to settle.

If you don't know where your documents are, you'll be leaving a mess for those who try to pick up the pieces when you are gone. We can help you coordinate and simplify your affairs through a written financial plan.

You will have daily access to an online financial center where all of your assets and debts, bank accounts and mortgages, and more are updated daily and matched with your financial plan. That's more than you can do with online money management software programs, because it's merged with your goals. You can see how the numbers correlate to what you want to do in life[4].

---

[4] Online Money Management Tools Fail To Deliver - Forbes October 15th, 2012

That means if you see a rising asset base over the next 30 to 40 years, you're doing everything you want to do, and then if the S&P should drop 200 points and have no effect on your overall plan, you can go outside and plant some flowers. Without that projection, you might turn on the financial news, hear about the crisis du jour, and worry yourself sick.

Once a year, we collect data from your financial center and create a "Total Client Profile™". It can be beneficial for whoever settles your estate someday.

Clients often wonder where they should keep such information. You might think a safe deposit box makes sense, but remember that the bank will close access to that box upon your death. It could take time and trouble for anyone to get at the information they need to settle your affairs.

We give our clients an online vault and scan everything into it, including wills and trusts and powers of attorney, property deeds, passports, birth certificates, and more. It's all in the vault. It's set up for access by your executor or trustee upon your passing.

Otherwise, you will at least want to create a document that lists everything important that you can bring to mind. There are online services that can help you, or just grab pen and paper and start writing. Who are your advisors? What are your assets and debts? Who carries your life insurance? Who should be contacted? What papers do you keep where? You'll want to keep that list with your will or trust papers, and perhaps give it to your executor or your children in advance. You can put copies of your insurance policies in the bank box, if you want—all the executor needs is the name of the insurer.

Whether it's your paperwork or your life that you are organizing, the process need not be complicated. But it is essential. You need perspective. You need a map for the rest of your life, with a clearly plotted route for what you want to see and do. If you don't have that map, you could be wandering in the dark, and that's no way to make it through Distribution Land.

{ CHAPTER THREE }

Finding Someone to Trust

Imagine that you have a 200-piece jigsaw puzzle scattered in front of you. Where would you start? When I ask people that, most say they would start at the corners where they figure it's easier to piece together all those interlocking shapes. Likewise, many people just dump their box of investments on an advisor's table and shift them around, trying this investment here, and that one there, and hoping that eventually things might fall into place.

But how about first taking a good look at the picture on the cover of the box? Before you start working on the pieces, you need to have the big view. You should work with an advisor who will make sure you get the perspective you need so that your investment strategy makes sense for you and is designed to advance your goals.

Actually, it is the picture on the cover of the box!

I recently met with a woman who had been widowed two years and wanted a second opinion about the financial products she had purchased. I looked at her portfolio and asked why so much of her money was tied up in a particular investment.

"Well, I told the man that I would need a retirement income, and how much, and this is what he put me in." The advisor did what she told him to do. He sold her stuff. It wasn't a wise allocation, but it met her request.

Is that why you want an advisor—to buy you stuff? Or do you want somebody to give you some direction? You wouldn't tell a captain how to navigate. You would depend on his knowledge about what is out there in the waters.

YOU NEED A PLANNER, NOT A SALESMAN

A lot of people in our industry sell stuff, but they may not do financial planning. By contrast, I strive first to understand my clients as people and their unique needs and dreams, and then I analyze the numbers and do an inventory of their finances to see if I can help them create a plan to pursue those aspirations. Not only do we draft the plan, but we also become stewards of it.

In my opinion, the financial planning industry in general tends to be good at dating, but less successful in marriage. You will find "advisors" who tell you what you want to hear just to get you as a client. Then they're in pursuit of someone else. We strive to provide diligent follow-up care—four quarterly meetings each year, preferably. The objective for each meeting is to reduce risks, focus on opportunities, and continue working so that we continue to tap into the client's strengths and stay true to his or her values.

Many people have an attorney whom they have seen occasionally, perhaps years ago when they had a will drawn up. And every March the accountant sends out a reminder to get those returns in on time, along with a friendly form letter. They may have advisors like that, who offer a tip or a quick fix, but what about doing any real planning or helping with the overall management of their finances?

There's no primary financial coordinator to help them through a life issue that could seriously offset their retirement hopes. That's my role. I tell my clients that my job is to decipher these issues for them and to talk them down off the ledge if I believe they are about to do something unwise.

Retirement planning may be more complicated than investing to accumulate assets. A good planner needs to analyze the client's expectations and finances and understand all the major risks that retirees face. As you head into retirement, you can search for somebody who cares about your unique situation.

And that somebody isn't likely to be the stockbroker who wants to direct you to all those hot mutual funds. The United States has about 1.3 million licensed stockbrokers and insurance agents, and they may call themselves financial planners, but there are only about 25,000 Certified Financial Planners™, or CFPs, who have completed the CFP® certification process.

According to a report by McKinsey & Company, 75 percent of respondents to a survey had switched or added advisors within 15 years of retiring, indicating that they considered retirement income planning to be important but couldn't get that service from most so-called advisors. The Fidelity Advisor 2010 Survey of Investors at Retirement found that 78 percent expected their advisor to create a plan to convert assets to cash flow, yet only 23 percent of the advisors did so.

People clearly want better service, but what they want may not be what is actually getting done. And a part of the problem may be that they are going to the wrong kind of advisors.

It comes down to this: If all you have is a hammer, then everything looks like a nail. Those who are licensed to do certain things are only going to do those certain things. Stockbrokers sell securities. People in the insurance business sell insurance products. They offer you what they know, but it might not be what you need. And what you may need in Distribution Land is an advisor who knows full well what you are likely to encounter there. You need somebody with different skills and tools than a typical Accumulation Land advisor possesses.

So, how can you quantify smart financial advice?

A new Morningstar approach may help you put a value on the value of an advisor.

In the wake of alpha, focused on picking individual managers, and beta, which looks at how much systematic stock market risk to take, researchers at Morningstar have devised what they're calling gamma to quantify the benefit planners can deliver to clients.

Gamma is defined as the additional value achieved by an individual from making more intelligent planning decisions. According to Morningstar, planners can add the equivalent of a 1.82 percent annual arithmetic return to clients through five components of gamma. Over time, that can translate to nearly 29 percent more that clients can spend in retirement.

Morningstar research executives David Blanchett and Paul Kaplan list five components of client service that make up gamma. (The table below spells out the payoff Morningstar expects from each element of its calculation.) None of these should come as much of a surprise to a good planner:

- Total wealth asset allocation

- Tax efficiency

- Dynamic withdrawal strategies

- Annuity planning

- Liability-relative optimization

If one or two of those terms seem opaque, you're not alone, so below are details on the actions and services planners should be providing to clients in each of the five areas, as well as a few others.

According to Morningstar, each of these components is worth a certain percent more each year and a cumulative amount over time. Here is the chart from the article:

CALCULATING GAMMA

Gamma Component	Income Generated	Equivalent Alpha
Total Wealth Asset Allocation	6.1%	0.38%
Asset Location and Withdrawal Sourcing	8.2%	0.52%
Dynamic Withdrawal Strategy	8.5%	0.54%
Annuity Allocation	3.8%	0.24%
Liability-Relative Optimization	2.2%	0.14%
Total	**28.8%**	**1.82%**

Source: Morning Star Direct

AN ABUNDANCE OF BAD ADVICE

You don't have to go far to find bad advice—or rather, advice that may be appropriate for someone else, but not for you. You need to know what to look for in a good retirement income advisor. Friends and associates may refer you to people they like, and if you go to the advisor's office you can assess whether he is wearing a nice suit or her office feels professional. But that doesn't tell you all that much. You need to come armed with a list of questions that will help you determine whether you are dealing with a salesperson or a true financial planner. If you have serious wealth, you want to find somebody who doesn't come with an agenda.

There are great stockbrokers and insurance agents who are ethical and do things right, so I'm not going to paint everyone with a broad brush. But be aware that those who work for the so-called wire houses have quotas to fill. They're in competition with one another, and they have products that they have to sell.

Some of my best friends are insurance agents and stockbrokers, so I understand the model. I hear their stories. Competition and performance requirements can drive them to aggressive action. They can get fired for lack of production. They are prohibited by regulation from selling away (selling things outside the scope of the firm). Along comes a retiree looking for the best investment for a specific need, and the agent or broker is more than willing to sell something appropriate. The question is: Appropriate for whom?

Some retirees are swayed by the financial news they watch on television or read in the journals or newspapers or even while surfing the Internet. Let me make this clear about the media: In my opinion, their aim is to scare you so that they get your attention, boosting ratings and readership. They need to keep their advertisers happy, and their fear is that if they tell you everything is great in the financial world, you might switch to a sitcom or turn to the comics pages.

I call it financial pornography—the media pander to what they think will attract your eyes. In my office, I have framed copies of Time Magazine covers from the 1980s and '90s. The big issues are recession and debt and other familiar woes. At a glance, you would think those were recent covers. The media recycles fear.

And what about Bob, who has so much financial scuttlebutt to offer over at the water cooler, or across the backyard fence? Have any of those to whom he dispenses such off-the-cuff wisdom ever taken a close look at Bob's personal financials? Some people look for advice in all the wrong places. Bob may be a great electrician, but it's unlikely that he understands the complexities of financial management in retirement.

I remember watching a Candid Camera program that showed people entering an elevator. If everyone on the elevator was facing left, the person entering the elevator joined them in facing left. If they faced right, he faced right. If everyone stood holding their hats, he took off his hat, too. People tend to follow the crowd. It's human nature.

DO-IT-YOURSELF DANGER

Others are die-hard do-it-yourselfers. I once asked an estate planning attorney how he got his best clients. "It's the people who try doing it themselves first," he answered. "They try to do their own planning, and I get more business by fixing things for people than I do from doing it right for them to begin with."

There can be a disconnect between having information and knowing what to do with it. Academics refer to the "pyramid of wisdom," at the base of which is data—the mass of facts and statistics surrounding us. Further refined, the data becomes information. Information can be processed into knowledge, and knowledge can lead to wisdom at the peak of the pyramid. But merely having access to information is no guarantee of knowledge or wisdom. You can read volumes about open heart surgery, but you wouldn't open your father's chest with a scalpel. You'd leave that to the surgeon who has reached the higher levels.

When it comes to investing, however, some people think that if they have obtained information, gleaned perhaps from the Internet, then they also have knowledge and wisdom. They generally do not. Investing wisely requires expertise and experience.

After the last market correction, a do-it-yourself investor came to my office. He wanted to hand over his portfolio.

"So why do you want to partner with me?" I asked. "Why do you want to stop handling this yourself?"

"It's just not fun anymore," he said. "It was fun when everything grew to the moon. Not anymore. So rather than me staying up all night worrying, I want you to stay up all night worrying." During the soaring market of the 1990s, some people thought they were smart as their portfolios grew. But a rising market isn't testimony to anyone's intelligence, and come the corrections, some people realized they need help. There's an old saying, "a rising tide floats all boats." Like the weekend warrior who made a mess of remodeling his bathroom, they recognize how easily they could muddle the job.

HOW IS YOUR ADVISOR PAID?

You need to understand how advisors make money so that you can weigh the advice that you receive. Some are paid commissions on products they sell. Some charge a fee for impartial service. Others make their money with a combination of commissions and fees.

Many advisors today are commission-based, a model that has long existed. If you buy something from them, they receive a fee for services based on a percentage of the dollar amount of the sale. That's how the majority of insurance products and investments such as mutual funds still are handled.

Some commission-based advisors state that you don't pay the commission; the company does. That would be true in a life insurance or auto insurance policy; you are going to pay the same price whether you get it from an advisor or you get it directly. For those types of products, it doesn't make a difference, so clearly you would want to work with an advisor.

As for those advisors who tell you that they work for you at no charge because their company pays the commission, ask yourself this: If they do all that work for you for nothing, how do they feed their kids and pay the mortgage? You have to buy something for the commissions to flow, and you may hear recommendations that will compensate them. You are putting yourself in a pressure situation.

Fee-based planners make their money by creating a financial strategy for you. Those who also sell products or manage assets would like you to implement that plan with them, but you are free to take the plan elsewhere to put it into action. Fee advisors have no ax to grind;in fact, their licensing requires that they act in a fiduciary capacity—that is, in your best interest as would be considered prudent according to a court of law.

That's why you may want to pay separately for planning services. The advisor has no vested interest or bias. He or she gets paid for the work, and you can implement the strategies as you please, if at all. You won't be pressured into buying or doing anything.

LOOKING FOR A GOOD ADVISOR

How, then, can you be sure whom you are dealing with? How do you know who will have that fiduciary responsibility to watch out for you? On my website, www.familywealthadvisory.com , you can download a report that will help you find the financial advisor who is right for you. It lists 16 crucial questions that you should ask before choosing your advisor.

Those with a designation of CFP (Certified Financial Planner) are required to follow a code of ethics. They will have passed certain exams like a Series 65; they may also be affiliated as a registered representative of a broker dealer; an investment advisor representative of a Registered Investment Advisor; or they could be independently registered as a Registered Investment Advisor. They are subject to regulation by various federal, industry, and state agencies.

In any case, if you were to have an advisor named, for example, Bernie Madoff, you don't want to see "Bernie's Excellent Investment Firm" stamped on your statements. You need to be aware of just who has your money. It seems like a simple thing, but people overlook this. You would want to have your money held by a custodian, like Pershing, LLC or Fidelity Institutional Wealth Services.

Nonetheless, ethical and unethical behavior cannot always be defined by a credential. There are examples of abuse of fiduciary responsibility in which CFPs lose their designation, but there are also many, many advisors without such licensing who are honest and dedicated to putting your interests first. How do you know who has your back? Your best choice is still to limit your risk and work with somebody with an obligation to abide by a code of ethics—a Certified Financial Planner.

Ask for a copy of the advisor's ADV Part 2B, a sample of which is in the report that you can download from our website. It will help you distinguish whether the advisor is fee-based or not. It's a disclosure form stating all the fees that the advisor can charge. If the advisor tells you he or she sees no need for a fee and will do the planning for nothing, ask to see the ADV Part 2B. An advisor who can't produce one is not allowed to charge an investment advisory fee; therefore, you may want to question the value of free.

The ADV Part 2B also discloses if there has been certain disciplinary history. There also are websites in which you can run checks for complaints against the advisor whom you are considering. I highly recommend that. On my website, www.familywealthadvisory.com, you can access a report with links, including those of the SEC (www.sec.gov/investor/brokers.htm) and FINRA (www.finra.org/Investors/ToolsCalculators/BrokerCheck/).

You should ask whether the advisor is an employee of a financial firm or working independently. Some advisors who work for a firm offer proprietary products, and they may have to sell certain products and meet minimums. Their primary objective may be to make money and limit their own risks.

Look instead for independent advisors. That doesn't mean they don't have relationships with certain firms, but they are paid as independent contractors. They are not salaried. Some independent firms have production requirements.

A good independent advisor acts on your behalf and knows you have unique needs and goals. Such an advisor will strive to establish a relationship, building rapport and trust, so that he or she knows you and understands what you seek in a financial plan. The advisor is interested in more than transactions and isn't out to sell you something. Instead, you will get a plan and a process for accomplishing it.

Ask to see the process. If the advisor can't produce one, or if it's all investment related and focused on money, be wary. What you want to see is a process that is centered on you, with the money there to support you.

A COORDINATOR FOR YOUR TEAM

By hiring a good advisor, you could be gaining a world of expertise; however, you should still feel firmly in control of your destiny. We designed our model, The WealthCare Process, from the world of business: You are the CEO or chief executive officer of your wealth. A good CEO hires a CFO or chief financial officer, who runs the daily affairs of the company—and we position ourselves as your CFO. We oversee and coordinate everything that requires planning and money with a written recommendation. We never take custody of your assets and you always have the final decision. We get to know your other advisors and their unique ability and then review any previous work done by them to make sure it is not in conflict with your present objectives. (For a detailed look at the Wealthcare Process, reference the Appendix on page 171.)

The goal is to have you feel free of financial worry so that you can spend your time focusing on what you enjoy. In my opinion, that's so much better than the old planning model in which you are in the middle, and circling around you like the moons of Jupiter are all of your current advisors: your CPA, who calls you up every March to ask you where your receipts are; your lawyer, whom you haven't seen in eight years since she handled your daughter's auto accident; and your insurance agent, who calls too much, always at dinner time. Then don't forget your investment advisor who hid under the desk in 2008 and wouldn't answer the phone. If you have such a "team," ask yourself when was the last time that they all got together and talked about your plan. In my experience, you'll find they are in their own orbits and may be offering conflicting advice.

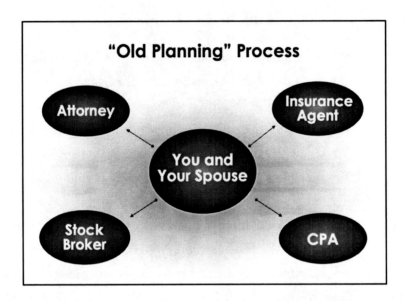

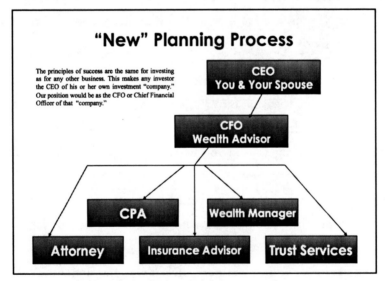

Of course, many do an excellent job, but if you find they only jump when you shout—if their idea of planning is reactive—then you may be better served with a primary financial coordinator to make sure that you are taking advantage of opportunities and are aware of dangers. How does a major change in your situation affect your taxes or your estate? How should you handle that? Is it time to see an attorney, or just your accountant? What are the financial ramifications of returning to work if, say, you get a great consulting opportunity? Are you overlooking an investment opportunity in which you can partake these days for a fraction of what it once cost to get in? Technology and economies of scale have been opening doors for smaller investors. And if you are truly affluent, are you taking advantage of what is available to you? I recently came across someone with $2 million in assets who was playing in a sandbox for $10,000 investors—putting his money in investments more suitable for smaller accounts, and therefore paying higher fees than would otherwise be necessary. He just didn't know what was available.

So many questions. If you have a constellation of advisors, each will see just a piece of the jigsaw puzzle. None of them is likely to help you know how to fit those pieces together. That's a job for a primary financial coordinator, who will work to keep the big picture in mind. You should expect regular communication. A good advisor will keep in touch so that you can make the adjustments to stay on course toward your goals. We can't change the wind, but we certainly can trim the sails.

You are still in control. You are still the CEO of your portfolio, and you have delegated the task of finding better solutions than you could uncover on your own. Some of the most successful people realize that others can do many things better than them. They surround themselves with such experts and direct them on what they want to accomplish. They are in control of their destiny, but they don't need to be orchestrating the details. Think of how a sports team operates. The owners don't hire and coach the players.

Entrepreneurs often feel driven to do it all themselves, as business coach Dan Sullivan points out. He calls it "rugged individualism," and it can be their downfall. It can be an investor's downfall, too. If you enjoy managing your finances and can do all aspects of it well, that's fine—you don't need me. But if you'd rather spend more time with your family or hobbies and passions, I am here as your guide in Distribution Land.

CHAPTER FOUR

So Much at Stake

Your sailboat is skimming across the water. The skies are blue, the seas calm, the wind is blowing at your back. You raise the sails high and wide and lean back with the beverage of your choice— perhaps a margarita. Times are good.

Suddenly, dark clouds rush toward you from the horizon. The water turns rough, the wind whips your face. Trouble is brewing, so you quickly furl the sails and begin rowing to regain control and maintain your course. It just makes sense, right?

The "buy and hold" strategy of investing, in essence, says the following: "Leave the sails up during the storm, because we'll soon have sunshine and pleasant breezes." Make sense? Not to me!

Not much has changed in the mainstream investment world in the last 30 years. Outdated strategies still are promoted as if the recent market storms never happened. Stay the course, some equity brokers say, or you'll miss the five best days. They don't mention the five worst days—what if you missed those? In truth, you may be better off missing some of the upside if you could drastically minimize the downside. People don't understand that.

Those who saw their life savings dwindle as the recession raged just a few years ago know full well how a retirement plan can be wrecked by the wrong strategy—if you can call that a strategy. "Buy and hold is a posture," says one of the portfolio managers with whom I work. "It's not a strategy." Some who were sitting on a million and thought they were set for life ended up going back to work.

For those who experienced investing from about 1982 to 2000, "buy and hold" did work; however, since the average age of a financial advisor is approaching 53[5], the math shows that most advisors don't have much experience prior to 1982. The expectation for years was that we would have a rising market with relatively brief bands of corrections. Advisors and investors experienced the greatest run-up of capital in world history, so staying the course made a lot of sense. And if you cut your teeth on that style of investing, you are likely to tell yourself, "It worked in the past. I'll do it again."

But the bull has given way to the bear. You can fight the bear, but you need the right kind of weapons. You can't treat it the way you did the bull, which you wanted to ride as long as you could. Strategies that worked in an up market may hurt you in a down or highly volatile market.

Furthermore, accepting more risk does not guarantee greater returns. Simply put, risk is not fertilizer; you don't spread it around and increase returns.

SAILING VS. ROWING

We use the analogy of sailing and rowing to explain how to manage money wisely. There are two strategies for sailing, when you

---

[5]The "Hidden" Issue Behind An Aging Advisor Workforce (7/3/2012)

are making the most of a favorable wind. There are two other strategies for rowing, when you are trying not to fall behind and lose your way in a storm. The rowing strategies aim to get a return through most market cycles. They are designed to manage the volatility better. A good portfolio is going to have a combination of all four of these strategies. On our website, you can watch a short video that illustrates the sailing and rowing analogy.

The two sailing approaches are called "strategic," which is the traditional buy-and-hold strategy, and "tactical constrained." The former calls for a fixed balance of stocks and bonds (for example, 60-40 percent) to weather any storm. The latter adjust those percentages depending on market conditions: In a volatile market, the balance may be 45-55. In a strong one, it may be 75-25. The adjustments are tactical, but they are constrained within boundaries. They can only go so far.

The two rowing strategies are "tactical unconstrained" and "absolute return." The former doesn't have those constraints that I just mentioned; the managers may decide to go 100 percent to cash in a highly volatile market, or may go 100 percent to equities if they are riding a trend upward. The latter is the strategy of the true rowers. They are looking to get a return of say, 2 or 3 percent above inflation during any market cycle, using such tactics as short selling and buying alternative investments.

Many investors will use a combination of those strategies, weighted toward whether their aim is to accumulate assets or preserve and distribute them. The balance of strategies also will depend on the market outlook and their risk tolerance—is the investor aggressive or moderately conservative? If you are an investor with a large account, you should meet with your advisor at least twice a year, preferably four times.

Together you can decide whether it is time to rebalance your strategies so that your portfolio remains in line with your goals.

A TRULY DIVERSIFIED PORTFOLIO

You probably have heard of the Rule of 100, which suggests that if you subtract your age from 100, the result is how much of your portfolio should be invested in stocks, with the remainder in bonds. Presumably, that would keep your investments diversified. However, that's not true diversification. If you have everything in stocks and bonds, you still have all of your assets exposed to some levels of risk.

In my opinion, rules of thumb such as that will generally hurt you more than they will help you because they are an attempt to apply a general principle to highly individual needs and wants. Should everyone age 76 have the same portfolio? Anyone suggesting so would be spouting hogwash. Everybody's situation is different. Some need more income than others. Life happens along the way. If you have a portfolio consisting of just stocks and bonds, "that's so 70s," as the saying goes.

The bond market is not a world of safety. Here's what people don't realize: We have just gone through a 30-year bull run in the bond markets.[6]

In 1981 you could get CDs for 16 percent; now, the rates are 1 percent or less. These are the lowest interest rates people have seen in their lifetime. Why were the bond markets so attractive in the last

[6] "PIMCO's Gross Says Bull Run in Bonds over." *Reuters.* Thomson Reuters, 10 May 2013.

30 years? Because as interest rates go down, the price of the bonds appreciate. It was a great place to obtain some safety and catch a wave for three decades.

Changing Interest Rate Environment

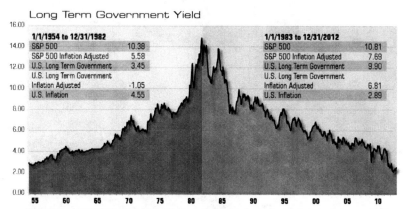

For illustrative purposes only. The information is not intended to be a recommendation to purchase or sell a security. Past performance is no guarantee of future results. Returns reflect reinvestment of capital gains and dividends, if any. Indices are unmanaged and do not incur fees. It is not possible to invest in an index. Stocks are represented by the S&P 500 Index. Bonds are represented by the Ibbotson Associates U.S. Long Term Government Index. Inflation-adjusted returns are based on the average Consumer Price Index (CPI) through the referenced period.

Source: Morningstar Direct

Today, with money market rates near zero, one could assume that rates cannot go down much further and that they likely will rise as some point in the future. As those rates rise, what will happen to bond values? They will fall. Rising rates equal falling bond value, just as falling rates equal rising bond value. Nonetheless, some people may be walking in the dark with their eyes wide open, thinking that because they are heavily into bonds, they are being conservative. A light is going to come on suddenly, and hopefully not too late.

A truly diversified portfolio isn't a mix of stocks and bonds, but rather it includes some genuinely conservative investments that were created for Distribution Land. These include insurance products. Professor Moshe Milevsky, a researcher, author, and speaker on personal financial planning, talks about not just asset allocation, but product allocation for retirement. We use an asset allocation chart created by Professor Milevsky that includes insurance annuities, life insurance, and other products.

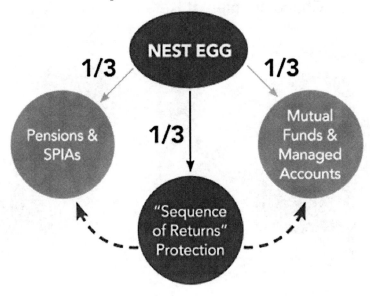

Source:

Product allocation is the next step in the evolution of asset allocation, designed specifically for people close to or in retirement. Rather than allocating a pool of money among asset classes, you also incorporate guaranteed income products.

According to Milevsky, product allocation can be accomplished with three product silos:

1. Traditional Investments: These could include separately managed accounts, exchange-traded funds (ETFs), mutual funds, and other conventional accumulation-based instruments.

Throughout retirement, one would systematically withdraw these assets, attempting to make them last as long as possible and then use asset allocation to achieve a desired return with an acceptable degree of risk.

2. Pensions and Immediate Annuities: These could include defined benefit plans and fixed income annuity products (or payout annuities). In exchange for fixed income payments, you give up liquidity, investment control, and in some cases, the ability to leave any of these assets to heirs.

3. Innovative Guaranteed Income Products: May offer income for life, exposure to stock market gains and losses, and control. They are also designed to leave remaining assets as an inheritance and can provide protection against sequence-of-returns risk.

How much money you should allocate to each category depends on your expected retirement age, gender, health status, desired spending rate, and inflation assumptions?

We will take a closer look in the next chapter on the above investment options as well as other investment options for a dependable retirement income.

HOW TO BLOW YOUR NEST EGG

I am in the business of managing risk. It's at the very heart of what I do. As you get closer to retirement, you need to insulate yourself from what the market can do to your portfolio, but you still need to have enough growth to keep in front of inflation and provide sufficient income to pursue your established goals.

If you don't take care, you can blow your nest egg. One way to do that is to ignore inflation. I meet with many clients who have trouble understanding that. They figure that if they can get a certain percentage off their account, they will be fine. I point out that they'll likely be living off that money for decades to come. Things will inevitably cost more; think of how much they cost in, say, the 1960s compared with now. A retirement plan should account for the need to have an income that keeps pace with inflation.

Making up for portfolio losses may be difficult

Impact of Volatility Five Hypothetical Portfolio Recovery Scenarios					
	1	2	3	4	5
Starting Balance	$1,000,000	$1,000,000	$1,000,000	$1,000,000	$1,000,000
Amount Lost	-$100,000	-$200,000	-$300,000	-$400,000	-$500,000
Remaining Balance	$900,000	$800,000	$700,000	$600,000	$500,000
Percentage Loss From Your Portfolio	-10%	-20%	-30%	-40%	-50%
What Would It Take to Recover Your Losses?	+11%	+25%	+43%	+67%	+100%

This is a hypothetical example used for illustrative purposes only and is not indicative of any particular investment. Chart created by Genworth Financial Wealth Management, Inc., which has authorized its use.

Source: Managing your portfolio with confidence – Genworth Financial Wealth Management, 6/21/2012

But if you do not manage risk wisely, an impressive portfolio can turn to a fraction of what it was, and rather swiftly. The millionaire next door can find himself back in that race he'd hoped to escape. You can be devastated by what is known as sequence of return risk. The mathematics is unforgiving: If you invest a dollar and lose half of it, you need a 100 percent gain to get back to a dollar. You won't overcome a 50 percent loss by following it with a 50 percent gain. That only gets you up to 75 cents. Some investors did suffer such percentage losses in 2008, and if they needed the account for systematic income withdrawals, it is highly unlikely they will ever recover.

We're in the middle of a long-term secular bear market. History has seen such cycles repeatedly: For 18 years, from 1906 to 1924, the market was flat. It was flat for 25 years from 1929 to 1954, and for 17 years from 1965 to 1982. The current slump started in 2000[7].

---

[7]Secular Stock Markets Explained S&P 500 Index 1900 - 2012– Crestmont Research

Copyright 2006-2014, Crestmont Research (www.CrestmontResearch.com)

Protecting your portfolio in down markets is as important as participating in up markets

Secular Bull & Bear Markets Jan. 1942 through Dec. 2012

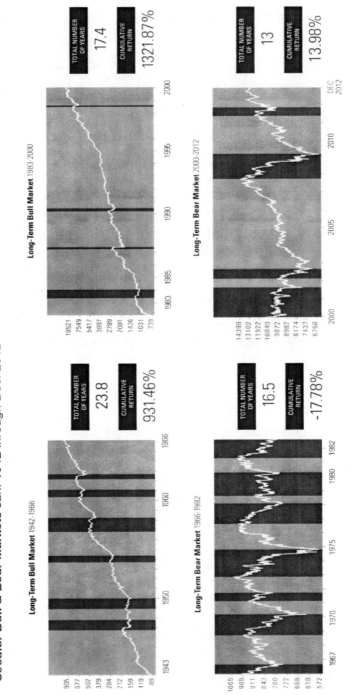

Source: Managing your portfolio with confidence – Genworth Financial Wealth Management, 6/21/2012

Sequence of return risk arises from those cycles of good years and bad ones. You cannot ignore it, particularly if you plan to retire now and will begin withdrawing money from your investments. You need to understand its potential to wreck your retirement plans. "Don't worry, you're fine," a misguided advisor may tell you. "Look here, your investment averaged 8 percent over the last three decades, so you can take out 5 percent and even increase it for inflation at 3 percent, no problem." But it's a big problem if you encounter some bad years early on.

For a detailed look at the sequence of returns, reference the Appendix on page 173.

A bad year or two may not have hurt you during the years when you made no withdrawals or were contributing to the account, because a good year or two could turn that around. Now, if those bad years come at the same time that you are siphoning money away for your income needs, the good years later on may not be able to overcome the hit—as the math demonstrates. The sequence of returns may do you in.

In your accumulation years, when you were adding dollars and buying equities at a bargain, you benefited from what is known as dollar-cost averaging: the technique of buying a fixed dollar amount of a particular investment on a regular schedule, regardless of the share price. More shares are purchased when prices are low, and fewer shares are bought when prices are high. Eventually, the average cost per share of the security will become smaller and smaller. Dollar-cost averaging lessens the risk of investing a large amount in a single investment at the wrong time.

For example, you decide to purchase $100 worth of XYZ each month for three months. In January, XYZ is worth $33, so you buy three shares. In February, XYZ is worth $25, so you buy four additional shares. Finally, in March, XYZ is worth $20, so you buy five shares. In total, you purchased 12 shares for an average price of approximately $25 each. Now, in retirement, as shares go down in value, you have to sell more of them from your account to obtain the same income. It's dollar-cost averaging in reverse. Think of it as dollar-cost *ravaging*.

Dollar Cost "Ravaging"
Selling More of Your Assets When Prices Are Low

GROWTH INVESTMENTS

TIME

Accumulation-
Creates Value

Decumulation-
Erodes Units

Accumulation
Buy Power Units

Decumulation
Sell Power Units

Accumulation
Buy More Units

Decumulation
Sell More Units

DON'T RISK YOUR DREAMS

Nonetheless, Wall Street and some advisors still put everything in a lump sum for systematic withdrawals. They will craft a portfolio that seems beautiful in its asset allocation, but really the income derives from withdrawing a percentage of the portfolio. And that puts the entire portfolio at risk.

Let's say it's in a 60-40 mix of stocks and bonds, and the market tumbles. "You don't have all your eggs in one basket," you will hear, and that's the line of "modern portfolio theory," which isn't so modern anymore, having been around for 60 years or so. It came from a time when the United States was the dominant investment player in the world. Today's global economy behaves differently. Someone drops a banana peel in Spain, and markets slip around the world.

Simply put, Modern portfolio theory tells you that your diversification leads to retirement success. But don't feel too reassured. In times of extreme volatility, investments get more closely correlated to one another. They start acting the same. It's as if a farmer went out to the barnyard and the pigs were oinking—and so were the chickens and the ducks and the cows. When everything oinks, there goes your diversity.

It's a risk you cannot afford, and we help you manage risks. We help with managing sequence of return risk as well as inflation risk. We manage downside risk, and there are a lot of proven ways to do that. The traditional model of asset allocation often works— but that's hardly a consolation to a couple who see their retirement dreams vanish during one of these times when it doesn't work—as in 2008 and 2002 and 2000. Knowing that what you tried should have worked isn't going to make you feel better when you are pinching pennies and heading back to work. An investment strategy that requires luck—luck that you will retire into a bull market and not a bear—isn't much better than a strategy that requires flipping a coin

Wall Street wants you to take that risk. It gets money from you whether you win or lose. The traditional investment strategies don't take into consideration that if you lose, your cash flow will suffer. You cannot accept that risk. There is too much at stake—you would be jeopardizing the retirement lifestyle that you dreamed about. We'll talk more about cash flow, and the necessity of a guaranteed income, in the next chapter. You need to know that you will be able to pay your bills, and you deserve to dream.

{ CHAPTER FIVE }

Money by the Bucketful

" I need a financial plan," the man said. So I explained that, yes, that's what I did, and that I could help him focus on goals and priorities and analyze his assets to see if we could work up a plan designed to provide income that would meet his needs for the rest of his life.

"That's not what I need," he said. "I don't need that stuff. I just want my money invested. See, I don't know if my wife and I have enough to retire."

"Why not?"

"Well, first off, I don't know how long we're going to live. I'm guessing I'll live to be 85, but people live a long time in my wife's family, so she'll make it to 95 at least. Unless she has a heart attack first—she's so stressed out. She's working nearly 80 hours a week. She needs to retire now."

"Do you have any plans for your retirement?"

"We want to live somewhere near the water. Not sure where. My wife wants to be near the kids, so we might go live there."

"And you say you're not sure you'll have enough money?"

"I think we will. That's the thing. It depends on what happens, and what we end up doing—and what if one of us gets sick? I need someone to invest what we have so I can know we will. I want somebody to work up the figures so I can prove to her we'll have enough coming in so she can retire now."

In further conversation, I discovered that they had some stocks, a pension, and Social Security. He had questions about whether he needed life insurance and long-term-care protection. He wanted, in other words, far more than investment help. He wanted help with his life. He was telling me, clearly, that he wanted a retirement financial plan that focused on establishing goals and income needs.

I often encounter that attitude. People want a retirement financial plan, but they just ask to have their money invested. They presume the advisor also will help them figure out whether they have enough to retire and meet their goals and whether they have their bases covered. It is my mission to do that for you—not just initially, but through the years as we monitor the plan. In my experience, you may have to look pretty hard to find an advisor who has the technical ability, resources, and support team that will do that for you. Getting your money for most of them is an event, not a process.

AN EMPHASIS ON INCOME

No doubt you have seen the acronym ROI, for return on investment. In Distribution Land, however, ROI stands for reliability of income. The conventional investment wisdom that may have served you well during your wage-earning years needs to be replaced with a more mature wisdom befitting this stage of life. You have a lot more to consider besides just the return you can get.

In the last chapter, we saw clearly how the recent lengthy bear market has dashed the retirement dreams of so many people. Simply stated, if you are drawing out money from an account as it is plunging, you will need an impossibly strong return the next year to break even again. Meanwhile, inflation may be silently eating away at the foundation.

It need not be that way. You can fight back with a strategy designed to anticipate the ramifications of your decisions. What you need is what many people lack: a written plan that forecasts retirement income and expenses to project how your savings can support your spending so that you can make intelligent decisions. And people need to talk through what they envision for retirement—where they want to be, why they want to be there, who they want to be there with. How do they feel about being retired? Do they have any concerns or fears?

A retirement plan isn't just about managing money. It has to coordinate your money with your life, and a good advisor can help smooth the way. The advisor has heard concerns like yours expressed many times. Creating a unique plan requires finding the right balance of hopes and dreams, the desired lifestyle, and the income needed to support it. It requires investing for a target income while still commanding a return that beats inflation. To get to the bottom of what people really want requires some finessing. And then you need to determine whether they are being realistic. If your asset base is relatively modest, you cannot take lavish vacations, support multiple charities, help all your children, play golf daily, and still have enough income for the rest of your life.

Retirement is no longer as simple as signing up for Social Security, collecting your pension, and sitting back. People are more active.

They live longer and work longer. With the extinction of most pension plans and the insecurity of Social Security, they have to rely more on what they have saved. That means that their income will need to last a lifetime and weather all storms: a health-care crisis, a recession, resurgent inflation, or whatever life throws at them.

SAFETY, LIQUIDITY, GROWTH: CHOOSE TWO

This might sound overwhelming, but it doesn't have to be. A retirement income plan has various components, each serving a different purpose, with an array of tools such as insurance products that can help where needed. You need the right toolbox for retirement income planning because it differs from investment planning. You need to build a solid floor of reliable income before exposing assets to the market.

A sound retirement plan must provide a good balance of safe, reliable income; of liquidity, so that cash is accessible in emergencies; and of growth, so that you beat inflation, grow your portfolio to replenish income needs, and leave an inheritance.

That's safety, liquidity, and growth, three fundamental aspects of money management. For any single investment, you can choose two. You can't have them all. In my opinion, it's similar to low price, high quality, and good service in the retail world. You can expect a maximum of two. A store offering low prices for brand products is likely to cut back on service. A luxury car dealer may provide first-rate service and quality vehicles, but you will pay dearly. A late-night offer for an incredibly inexpensive widget might arrive at your doorstep in a day, but how long before the widget wobbles?

Liquid investments may include cash, savings, and money market accounts. Low-risk investments may include short term bonds, insurance products, and bank certificates of deposit. Slightly more aggressive, but still reasonably conservative choices, include fixed income investments, such as corporate or government bonds. Growth investments could include individual stocks and real estate, for example.

BEWARE THE DEPRESSION MENTALITY

Few of us need to access all our money at any one time, so we give up some liquidity—that is, most of us do. A woman once came to my office and opened her checkbook, telling me she had about $300,000 in her account. I asked why she felt she needed that much in a checking account.

"I have it there for emergencies," she explained.

"I could be wrong, but that would be more like a national disaster than an emergency," I said. "What could possibly happen that you would need that much money?"

I wanted her to see that she was squandering potential. Few people could need immediate access to that much cash. The price of liquidity is a low rate of return, and low growth means that inflation may overtake you. Some people can't visualize that, because they lack a written retirement income plan that spells it all out. If their income suffices for now, they figure that it always will, even as prices creep ever higher. They sacrifice growth for liquidity even though, for the most part, they don't need it.

"A dollar doesn't buy what it used to buy," my grandmother often said. Now I know what she meant and why she was saying it; she still had the same dollar, as the years went by, and was simply living off the interest. Such was the Depression mentality: Some of those who endured hard times held on so tightly to their money that they sacrificed growth and eventually succumbed to the ravages of inflation.

CALCULATING YOUR INCOME NEEDS

In the process of retirement income management, the key is finding the right balance that suits the retiree. The individual's unique circumstances will determine how much investment risk is appropriate and tolerable and how much of the mix should be liquid or kept safe.

The first step is to estimate how long a retirement income will be needed. How many years must the assets last? Are you and your spouse healthy? Is there a history of longevity in your family? The next step is to identify and manage the numerous risks that the retiree may be facing, and then to reduce as much as possible the estate and distribution taxes.

After assessing all those factors, we can then start to convert resources into income, regularly updating the plan. Converting assets for lifetime income is the fundamental strategy in the retirement income planning process.

One approach is to make sure that at least your essential, basic expenses, such as food, clothing and housing, are covered by reliable income sources. Social Security and pension and other streams are unlikely to dry up. Other sources of income can then be developed to pay for discretionary expenses like travel, entertainment, and club memberships. These managed income sources can include taxable accounts, personal retirement accounts, and employment income.

Creating a Retirement Income Plan

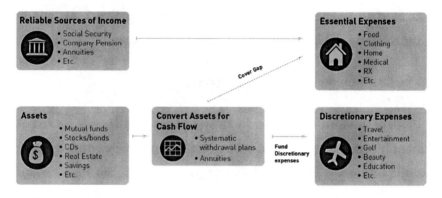

This is the layman's approach to calculating income needs: (1) figure average monthly expenses, (2) add up any lifetime income such Social Security and pension, and (3) subtract the monthly income from the expenses to determine any gap. To see if the gap can be filled, add up all financial assets and multiply by an expected annual rate of return, then divide the result by 12 for a monthly income stream. If it fills the gap, you can retire.

If it doesn't fill the gap, look at some other approaches. You have various options: Increase your returns where possible; find other lifetime income sources; spend less in retirement; work full or part time; postpone the start of Social Security or pension payments; increase your savings; or tap into your home equity.

Reverse mortgages may be one option for retirement income. It's not a wise move for everyone, nor is it bad for everyone. It depends on the situation. Where a reverse mortgage is applicable, it works. There certainly has been a lot of abuse, but legislation[8] has made the process considerably less expensive in the last several years.

Many retirees have fortunes locked up in their homes, and sometimes they have to tap into that equity because of their longevity. As baseball legend Mickey Mantle said: "If I'd known I was gonna live this long, I'd have taken a lot better care of myself."

INCOME STRATEGIES

Many advisors still subscribe to systematic withdrawals for retirement income, in which you take a certain percentage annually from a pile of money. How much is safe to withdraw? You hear various amounts, such as 4 percent. But the tactic of withdrawing from an account that rises or falls with the market can be debilitating to your wealth, as explained earlier. You are at the mercy of sequence of return risk and reverse dollar-cost averaging. If those don't drain your account, you will most likely deplete it entirely just by living too long.

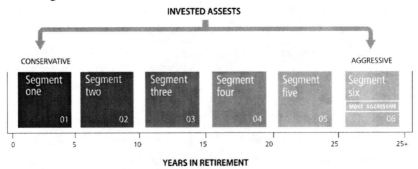

Systematic withdrawals would need to come from a highly diversified portfolio to reduce exposure to the market's fluctuations. But

---

[8]Source: Reverse Mortgage Stabilization Act of 2013

that "diversification" too often is defined as stocks and bonds and cash. The portfolio doesn't include alternative investments or any downside protection strategies. Alternatives, as an asset class, are favored mainly because their returns have a low correlation with those of standard asset classes. Alternative investments are designed to move independently of the broader market. Adding alternative investments to a traditionally diversified portfolio may provide the potential to capture a portion of market gains, while potentially limiting losses when the market experiences a downturn. A lot of the systematic withdrawal strategies are plain vanilla.

An effective strategy could be to use annuities. However, you might not want those products to make up all of your portfolio; because of costs and liquidity issues, you might be better served having them only as a portion.

A more disciplined structure for creating retirement income is called the time segment of allocation model. Basically, this approach is designed to spread your portfolio across multiple accounts, each designed to produce income over a certain period of time. How each account is invested depends on how soon the money is to be used. They may make use of a variety of asset classes and investment companies and product lines. Typically, the initial segments are for immediate needs and may therefore be allocated conservatively in fixed rate or even guaranteed investment products such as certificates of deposit or immediate annuities that may not be subject to a fluctuation in principal.

Segments designated for later use can be invested more aggressively. Since they won't be touched for a while, they have time to overcome market corrections. That approach helps to reduce the sequence of return risk, which Dr. W. Van Harlow, director of investment retirement solutions at Putnam Investment Management, identifies as the greatest risk to a retiree's portfolio. If you are depending on the markets for success, he says, it is crucial to find a way to protect yourself from the volatility.

EMOTIONAL RISKS

All investments have tradeoffs. You just can't have it all. Very often we find that retirees want safety of principal first, as one would expect. Let's face it; if you need to take risk because you haven't accumulated enough money, then you probably shouldn't be retired. But the big question is, once you decide that your priority is safety, should you still pursue some growth and have liquidity?

Giving up liquidity does not mean you can't touch your money at all. The risk, known as "Liquidity risk," is the risk that a given investment cannot be bought or sold quickly enough to prevent a loss or minimize a loss. Additionally, some investments have tax consequences when sold and may also have a surrender charge, which is a fee you incur when you sell, or cancel, certain types of investments or annuity policies. You may still experience growth, but you may need to limit your annual distributions to a reasonable percentage. Otherwise, you should consider safety products with guarantees.

Some individuals who are interested in safety and income may find that guaranteed income products are appropriate for their needs. While these products have their benefits, they may also come with some drawbacks. Therefore, very careful consideration must be given prior to deciding whether these are appropriate. In this section, we will examine some of the characteristics of guaranteed income products as well as some of their benefits and drawbacks.

WHAT IS A GUARANTEED-INCOME PRODUCT?

There are two main types of guaranteed income products. The first of these, often referred to as an annuity, is essentially a product where, for an initial investment, an individual receives a guaranteed income stream for the remainder of his or her life. Annuities can be further broken down into fixed-rate products. A fixed-rate annuity guarantees a certain level of income for the term of the annuity; however, it is possible that inflation will gradually eat away at the value of the income stream.

The second main type of guaranteed income product is the reverse mortgage. In a reverse mortgage, homeowners receive monthly payments from the reverse-mortgage lender for the remainder of their lives. At the time of their death, the money they have received must be repaid to the lender by the estate, or possession of the house is granted to the lender. The decision to take out a reverse mortgage can be a difficult one to make. The AARP, an American organization dedicated to protecting the elderly and retired, has extensive free resources designed to educate senior citizens about potentially unjust lending practices. Anyone considering a reverse mortgage should gather as much information as possible before carefully deciding whether a reverse mortgage is appropriate.

BENEFITS OF GUARANTEED-INCOME PRODUCTS

Guaranteed-income products can essentially function like a pension plan by providing consistent monthly income payments to retirees in order to help individuals plan their cash flow needs during retirement. Guaranteed-income products may also make budgeting simpler because monthly cash flow is known in advance and is not dependent on financial market conditions.

DRAWBACKS OF GUARANTEED-INCOME PRODUCTS

While stable income for life is an enticing proposition, guaranteed-income products do have several disadvantages. One of these disadvantages is that individuals are generally locked into a relatively low rate of return. In other words, if an investor buys a diversified stock and bond portfolio instead of purchasing a fixed rate annuity, portfolio growth over time may ultimately provide a higher level of income than the annuity offers. This means that in exchange for a guarantee of safety and income an individual sacrifices the possibility of higher returns. Costs can also be high with guaranteed income products, or are not always readily apparent, and guarantees are based on the claims paying ability of the issuing company. This makes comparison shopping absolutely vital when considering these products.

A second drawback of guaranteed-income products is that they often suffer from a lack of liquidity. In other words, once an individual has committed to an investment in a guaranteed-income product they may not be able to reverse their decision. As well, these products may not keep pace with the rate of inflation. In other words, the income the individual receives may gradually be worth less in real dollar terms as time goes by. Some newer guaranteed-income products offer protection against this in the form of cost-of-living adjustments; however, it is important to remember that the investor does not get something for nothing. Future cost-of-living adjustments are priced into the cost of the product.

Guaranteed-income products are also unattractive options if an individual dies at an early age. The longer the individual lives, the more annual income payments they receive, and the higher the "return" on their initial investment. An early death results in fewer income payments, and therefore a less attractive investment return. Therefore, general health and life expectancy are important considerations prior to purchasing a guaranteed-income product. It is also important to determine whether a spouse is going to be included in the guaranteed-income contract; if so, plans should be made for the annual income payments to continue as long as either spouse is alive.

Finally, guaranteed-income products may not be appropriate options for individuals interested in leaving a bequest to their heirs. Individuals interested in providing for future generations might be better off building a traditional investment portfolio, spending what is necessary during their lives, and then leaving the remainder to their heirs.

What we want individuals to do is seek to identify, understand, and manage risk by focusing on investment vehicles that offer a higher potential for lower volatility, better downside protection, and consistent compensation for the risk they are taking. They often are not focusing on lower volatility and downside protection. They're just focusing on higher potential return.

They easily can get caught in emotions. There's an old saying in the industry that if you want to have a Morningstar two-star investment in the future, buy this year's five-star investment. That's what most people do. We call it rearview mirror investing.

On the way up, they go from optimism, to excitement and exhilaration, to euphoria—and that's the point of maximum risk. On the way down, they go from anxiety to denial to panic to despondency—and that's the point of maximum opportunity. Unfortunately, it's also where most people bail out. But then the cycle starts anew.

THE EMOTIONAL INVESTMENT CYCLE

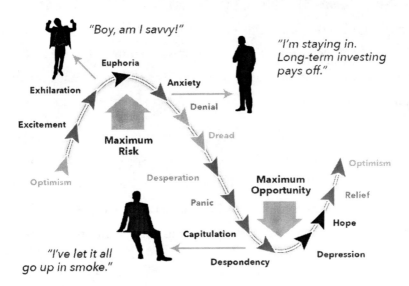

In a White Paper by Aftcast in 2010 titled "Lifelong Retirement Income: Cost of Excluding Variable Annuities," an analysis of market performance over the past century showed that extreme changes represent only about 3 percent of the time line. In other words, what has made money for investors have been the extremely good markets that happen only 3 percent of the time, and what created catastrophic losses happened only 3 percent of the time. But when those times hit, emotions run high. Investors feel they are missing the boat and come in to the market just before the peak, setting themselves up for loss. Or they panic and bail out, fearing they are losing everything, just before that trend turns around.

That's why it is important to work with an advisor who will work with you to help avoid the big mistake and keep your emotions from getting the best of you. People sometimes panic and pursue high-risk interest rates, believing that is their only choice if they are to survive. It's not the case. If you have a written retirement income plan, you will be able to see that.

What you need is a rate of return that is appropriate for your goals. That's the target you should pursue, not the S&P index. And you need the right balance of income sources that you can depend upon. They can be a mixture of guaranteed sources, non-guaranteed sources, and protection products. Guaranteed-income sources include Social Security, defined benefits, maybe annuity payouts. Non-guaranteed investments are stocks, bonds, mutual funds, and CDs—and I include CDs because they aren't there forever and rates change. Protection products[9], such as a guaranteed lifetime annuity, life insurance, disability, and long-term-care insurance answer questions such as what you will do if you live too long, pass away, get sick, or need long-term care. It's important to consider all those income sources and see if they cover your goals and the issues you will face in retirement.

WHEN TO COLLECT SOCIAL SECURITY

Determining when to begin taking Social Security benefits has a big impact on a client's long-term financial strategy. It requires a complex analysis of retirement income goals.

---

[9]All guarantees are based on the claims paying ability of the issuer.

[10]by Jane Bryant Quinn, AARP Bulletin, October 2013

About half of all people who file for Social Security do so early at age 62[10]. And for many, that is a really costly mistake. And why are they doing it? They are doing it because everyone else is doing it. And they are doing it because they want the money as soon as they can get it.

The main value of Social Security is the replacement of current income, not an accumulation of assets. Many people don't realize what a significant difference delaying the benefit could make.

The benefit needs to be considered in the context of the family, not individually. If both you and your spouse work, each of you is potentially eligible for benefits based on your individual work record. Your spouse is also eligible for benefits based on your work record. And if either of you dies, the survivor can collect a benefit as well. There's a lot going on there. A wrong decision on Social Security can end up costing a retiree a couple hundred thousand dollars in lost benefits. That's not chump change. Deciding when to begin collecting Social Security benefits is one of the most important retirement income decisions you will have to make.

In most cases it makes sense to wait until your normal retirement age[11], and currently that's at 66 for anyone born from 1943 through 1954, and increasing to age 67 for those born in 1962 and after.

If you wait until your normal retirement age, two things happen. You are no longer subject to the earnings cap, meaning you can continue to work without jeopardizing any of your Social Security income, and you can get creative with your collection strategy to maximize your benefits. I have had clients who were amazed to hear

---

[11]When to Claim Social Security Benefits - by Jane Bryant Quinn, AARP Bulletin, October 2013

that they could collect Social Security while also working and getting a pension.

Below is a hypothetical example of one such creative strategy for maximizing benefits.

Here's how it works. At 66, one spouse can file and suspend, triggering spousal benefits for the other and delaying his/her own retirement benefit until 70. Then, the other spouse, at 66, should file a restricted claim for spousal benefits only and delay collecting retirement benefits until 70. The couple will end up collecting one spousal benefit at 66 and two maximum retirement benefits at age 70.

Let me give you an example of how the numbers work. Say both spouses are entitled to $2,000 per month at their normal retirement age of 66. When the husband turns 66, he can file and suspend his retirement benefit, triggering a $1,000-per-month spousal benefit for his wife. At 66, the wife can file a restricted claim for spousal benefits only, collecting the $1,000-per-month spousal benefit rather than her full $2,000 retirement benefit.

Because they have both deferred their own retirement benefits, each will continue to accrue delayed retirement credits worth 8 percent per year between their normal retirement age of 66 and age 70. In this case, each of the $2,000-per-month retirement benefits at normal retirement age will increase to $2,640 per month by age 70. At that point, they each would switch to collect their enhanced benefits

---

[12]Make the Most of Social Security – Kiplinger, March 2012 | By Mary Beth Franklin

In the above example, their combined Social Security benefits would total $5,280 per month at age 70. That's more than $63,000 per year in guaranteed income for life and their larger base amount would translate into larger cost-of-living adjustments in the future. But a word of caution: They both can't claim spousal benefits, and one spouse must take action to trigger benefits in order for the other spouse to claim them.

Another tip: If you are receiving benefits and have a dependent under 18 in your household, the child is also entitled to monthly benefits worth up to half of yours. This often is the case when an older filer has a child in a second marriage. Some call this the Social Security Viagra strategy[12].

We can help you with such questions. We have a guide on when is the best time to start collecting Social Security, as well as creative claiming strategies you probably didn't know you could do. It's called "A Baby Boomer's Guide to Social Security." We also offer a free report called "**GOOD DECISIONS: Getting the Most from Social Security**." You can download these on our website, www.reliabilityofincome.com.

YOUR INCOME INVESTMENT BUCKETS

After you have clearly defined your goals for retirement and how much income it will take to reach them, it's time to set up the strategy that can make it all happen. Such a strategy addresses your short-term needs while pursuing sufficient growth to offset inflation and realize your long-term goals.

A time segmented model of income planning divides the client's assets into five-year increments. You can think of these as buckets for your money. Each bucket is funded with enough money in appropriate investments to provide an income for that period of retirement.

In retirement, as I mentioned, ROI stands for reliability of income[13], a far greater concern in these years than return on investments. You can't effectively chase both at the same time. But you can pursue both goals if you compartmentalize your money based on short-term, medium-term, and long-term goals.

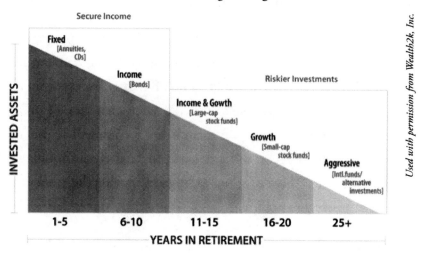

You may have seen what is called the "risk pyramid," rising from conservative fixed investments at the bottom to more aggressive growth vehicles at the top. Imagine that pyramid toppled on its side. You would have, at the left, the widest part—the fixed investments. At the right you would have the growth investments. This pyramid on its side is another way to visualize the time sequences in this type of income planning. At the left are the investments for immediate income. At the right are the investments that will grow, untouched for now, for later use. They will serve to replenish your income needs as time goes by.

---

[13] *ROI Reliability of Income* is a registered trademark of Wealth2k, Inc. Used with permission.

HERE'S HOW IT WORKS:

Using sophisticated computer technology, we look at your income requirements. We input your reliable sources of income such as Social Security, perhaps a pension, and reliable sources such as income from a job. Then we put in the targeted growth rate, and we use conservative figures. If we end up with a higher rate, that's better, but we want to make sure we're not taking a risk in the early years.

Then we set up four to six segments, usually in five-year payout periods. The first bucket takes you to five years into retirement; the second takes you to ten years; and so on. The early buckets contain more conservative investments, and the later ones can be more aggressive because the money in them is not for immediate use. As the early buckets are spent, the later ones progressively are liquidated to replenish them. Think of a bucket brigade, moving the money up the line to where you need it.

The first phase focuses on reliable income. With limited income choices these days, an appropriate investment in this bucket may be a five-year immediate payout annuity, fixed income securities, or some form of bond or CD ladders.

Laddering a CD portfolio is a lot like dollar-cost averaging when you buy equities. You don't invest all your CD money at one low rate of return.

You also are never more than a year away from at least some of your money.

HERE'S HOW LADDERING CDS WORKS:

You go to the bank with $25,000 and buy a $5,000 one-year CD, a $5,000 two-year CD, and so on until your last $5,000 buys you a five-year CD. Each year is a rung on the ladder. When the one-year CD matures, you reinvest that money in a five-year CD because by that time your five-year CD has four years left until it matures. As each year's CD comes due, you roll it into a five-year CD.

The second phase—the bucket for years six through ten—focuses on conservative income-generating investments such as a deferred annuity that can be converted to an income annuity. Segment two could be some fixed annuity products, CDs, or even managed portfolios. The goal here is to refill the immediate income bucket every five years.

Segment three could be fixed annuities, fixed indexed annuities, as well as managed accounts, which could comprise individual equities, fixed-income securities, and ETFs.

Then, when you get out to buckets four, five and six, you are basically using either types of individual equity portfolios or managed account portfolios, depending on the investor, the advisor, and the individual's choice.

You can see that as you get more out into space and time, and you get to that 15-year period and beyond, that's where your more aggressive investments are. Such a strategy is designed to minimize the risk of the money you will need sooner while also striving to manage risk in later years. In the early stages, the money's in low-risk investments. Later accounts may face risk, but the money in them will have time to possibly recover any losses.

This amounts to spreading out your portfolio into several piles that are invested according to when they will be needed. It's a far different strategy than tapping into one big pile that is at the mercy of the market. And by now, before it's too late, I hope you can clearly see the potential negative consequences of keeping all your money in one bucket.

YOUR CASH FLOW BUCKETS

Finances are a major source of stress for couples. One spouse may be spending too much, and the other resents it. Neither may know where the money is going. This program gives them power over their finances and the opportunity to live a life unencumbered by financial worry. Toward that end, it sets up a "bucket" system for managing money.

The First Step Cash Management system allows cash to flow into three accounts or "buckets." Each of the three buckets holds a specific type of money, and each type of money has a specific use or purpose. While the uses are all different, all three buckets are interrelated.

Your Three Buckets of Money

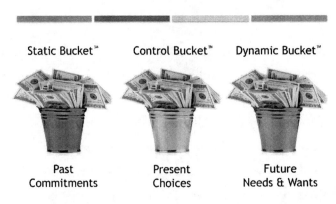

Static Bucket™	Control Bucket™	Dynamic Bucket™
Past Commitments	Present Choices	Future Needs & Wants

The Static Account™ bucket holds money that has been spent or has been agreed to be spent at some point in the past.

Static expenses include both long-term debt such as mortgage, home equity loans, student loans, and auto loans; and short-term debt such as credit cards, insurance, taxes, and utilities.

The Control Account™ bucket contains money that will be spent within the next seven days. Control expenditures include things such as groceries, entertainment, pet care, clothing, and personal maintenance.

Lastly, the Dynamic Account™ bucket stores money that will be spent in the future on things such as charitable giving, debt reduction, vacation, and gifts.

According to an AARP study[14], more retirees fear running out of money than they fear death. For retirees who feel overwhelmed by the many decisions they face as they enter retirement, a bucket strategy may help them divide what they see as one large stress-inducing problem into smaller, more manageable pieces. It links portions of money directly to goals. This can give retirees more of a feeling of control because it allows them to create a sustainable income stream from a large pool of assets, and that can be a daunting task. Creating a strategy for retirement can inspire confidence and reduce stress.

The First Step Cash Management System™[15] developed by The Planning Center and distributed by Money Quotient.

---

[14]Running Out of Money Worse Than Death - by: Carole Fleck: AARP Bulletin, July 1, 2010

[15]First Step Cash Management is owned by The Planning Center Inc. and Distributed by Money Quotient, NP

YOU DESERVE TO SLEEP BETTER

You may not even need all your life savings to set up an income plan—so why in the world would you consider putting it all at risk? The only thing you can do is screw it up.

"I want to take $50,000 out of this account and take the family to Italy," a client told me recently. "I'm turning 65, and you never know, it's a once in a lifetime thing. Do you think it's a good or a bad idea?"

"Well, that is a lot of money for a vacation."

"I know, but that's not what I'm asking. Is it appropriate based on the amount of money we have?"

For someone who may still be working, delaying Social Security, doing all the right things,

Should this inheritance have possibly been used to help them make some memories, or to make him the richest person in the cemetery?"

How many people out there are not sleeping at night, trying to figure out such matters on their own? They need a written retirement income plan, and they need an advisor who knows what's what in Distribution Land.

{ CHAPTER SIX }

Facing down the Enemies

As you near retirement, it can feel as if you are climbing Mount Everest and just need to hold on long enough to reach the summit. Once there, you hope to behold that glorious view of Distribution Land shimmering below you, stretching out to the horizon.

It has been a long and tiring trek on the front slope of the mountain, in Accumulation Land. You faced a mountain of obligations, above and beyond saving for retirement, and now you wonder if you are anywhere near the peak. And when you make it, will you be able to see clearly what lies beyond. Or will the mist be so thick that for all you will know you never left the base camp?

Nonetheless, you have made it this far, and you are determined to forge onward. But consider this: A great many of those who have perished on Mount Everest met their fate on the descent, not the ascent. A mountain climber needs an entirely different set of skills on the way down.

Some people need a competent guide on both sides of the mountain—someone who has been there many times before and knows the terrain and conditions. Otherwise, a sudden change in the weather or the wind could do you in.

A financial advisor can create a strategy designed to help you come down the slope safely, inspire a sense of accomplishment, eager for the next challenge. You can be sure there will be many challenges in Distribution Land. There are dangers there, but my hope is that this book will equip you with the tools and weapons and skills that you may need not only to cope but to flourish so that you can truly enjoy the scenery.

In this chapter, let's take a closer look at some of the enemies in Distribution Land—that is, the specific risks to a retiree's portfolio. I've introduced you to some of them already, such as sequence of return risk and inflation, but there are more—and two of them in particular are so troubling that I will be devoting a chapter ahead to each of them. One of them is this: What happens if you get sick or need long-term care? The other: What if the current status of IRA and 401(k) accounts changes in the future?

Here are the threats I want to make sure will not surprise you:

- Sequence of return risk

- Inflation and interest-rate risk

- Bond market risk

- Tax issues

- Fees for probate

- Health-care and long-term care needs

SEQUENCE OF RETURN RISK

The sequence of return risk, which I explained in Chapter 4, is one of the enemies you could find in Distribution Land, and it's crucial for a retiree to understand what can happen. You need to be able to clearly identify this threat.

To recap what this danger is all about: When you were younger, you may have contributed regularly to your portfolio, confident that despite market swings, the price would rise by retirement time. Now, in retirement, you may not be adding shares; instead, you sell them for income, and if the market dips you may have to sell even more to maintain that income. You may have fewer remaining assets to compound, and you don't have years to make up for losses. Once, you had a long time to accumulate money, and time was on your side. Now, you may have to live off your money a long time, and time may not be an ally, but rather a foe.

It's true that your investment's rate of return over the years might still average a respectable percentage, even as you are suffering. How could that be? It's because the rate of return is measured simply as an average over the years. Some are good years, some less so. But if you hit a string of bad years early in your retirement, the average will be little consolation. Welcome to the concept of sequence of return risk. Early losses can be next to impossible to overcome.

Mistakes can be disastrous to your financial well-being at this stage. During the accumulation phase, if you make mistakes in planning, saving, or investing, you may be able to fix them by adding more money—working longer, revising the portfolio, whatever it takes. In retirement, the money is coming out and there may be no new money going in. There's far less room for error, and it's a huge error to subject your entire pile of money to sequence of return risk. As we saw in the last chapter, there may be better way.

Remember: It's on the trip down the mountain that climbers are more likely to meet their demise. This is the endgame. When people realize they simply cannot risk screwing up at this point, a financial advisor could help provide guidance for their unique situations.

INFLATION RISK

To some degree, everyone is aware that prices of most items go up. We understand intuitively that things will cost more in the future than they cost today. But few people have a full understanding of the impact that inflation will have over long periods of time.

In 1960, my parents bought their home in New Jersey for $13,000. We sold it nearly half a century later, after both had passed away, for about a quarter of a million dollars. Imagine if the real estate agent, standing on the sidewalk with them back then, had suggested it would be worth that someday. They would have thought of her as a lunatic. Think of what your home is worth today. Can you imagine it selling for 20 times that much? It would seem unfathomable. But it's just one example of the ever-increasing cost of things.

In 1949, a gallon of gas cost 27 cents. You could dine out for $2 in 1950. A ticket to the World Series in 1964 cost $12, and a postage stamp cost 6 cents in 1970[16]. Compare any of those with today's prices, and you see the problem with inflation. It has been called the silent killer.

Suppose you had a hundred dollars in your pocket in 1900 and were magically transported to 2013. Your money would be worth $3.68. Likewise, $10,000 would be worth $368 today. A millionaire would be reduced to $36,800. Inflation has averaged a moderate 3 percent since 1900, yet look at what it has done to purchasing power.

Assuming that the average rate of inflation continues for another 20 years—say, between age 65 and 85—the value of a hundred dollars will be cut almost in half. For a typical couple, at least one spouse will live three decades or more in retirement.

Through your working years, you likely got regular raises that kept pace with inflation. In retirement, you have to create your own raises. Your assets need to grow. It's a simple matter: You either grow your money, or you spend the principal—one or the other.

---

[16]wiki.answers.com

In 1981, CD rates were about 16 percent. If you had a million dollars to invest in 1981, you got $160,000 in income. You were living large and probably bragging about those CDs, even though a double-digit inflation rate was eating away at your return.

Over the years, those CD rates have declined, and today they are about 1 percent. A million-dollar investment now pays out only $10,000 in income. At the same time, inflation has continued to increase the cost of living.

Suppose you took a job in 1981 that paid $160,000, and today, that same job paid you only $10,000. Do you see a problem with that? Are you bragging about that job? Well, if you wouldn't take that job, why in the world would you give your money a job like that? What people don't realize about CDs is that they have just about never outpaced inflation.

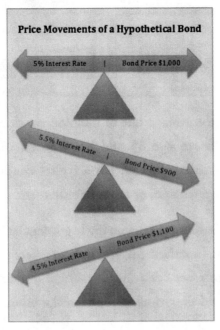

"Duration—What an Interest Rate Hike Could Do to Your Bond Portfolio." Investor Alert. FINRA.

http://www.finra.org/Investors/ProtectYourself/InvestorAlerts/Bonds/P204318 [Accessed 10-June-2013]

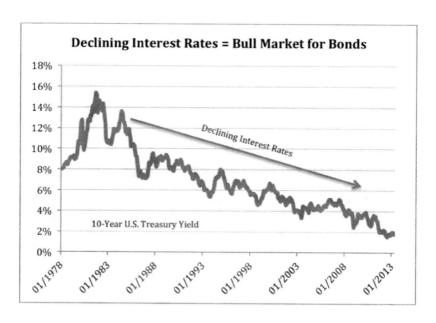

Declining Interest Rates = Bull Market for Bonds

Declining Interest Rates

10-Year U.S. Treasury Yield

www.sentryretirement.com/wp-content/uploads/2013/07/bond-alert.pdf

After peaking at above 15 percent in 1981, the yield on 10-Year Treasury Bonds has been in decline, reaching a historic low of near 1.38 percent in July 2012.

Although it is impossible to know for certain, many economists believe that interest rates will begin to rise in the near term, putting downward pressure on bond prices.

However, it is a mistake to conclude that inflation is so troubling that you must take big investment risks to tame it. That's no way to manage the problem. Some people tend to think, "I've got my nest egg now," and want to guard their pile. They thought CDs were safe, and when they hear about the inflation risk, they figure they are being told the only alternative is to plunge it all into stocks. And that's because they're thinking of their nest egg as a single pile. As we discussed in the last chapter, you may be able to manage the risk by dividing the money up into time segments. In my opinion, with professional management, you can have a higher probability that your portfolio will provide the income you need and the growth that fights inflation.

BOND MARKET RISK

A lot of people who think they have their life savings conservatively invested in bonds may be in for a big shock. They think that bonds are a safe haven because their prices have risen for 30 years as interest rates have fallen. But those rates may have hit bottom. Today's investors have little experience with what that means, although there have been price dips that should have served fair warning. You can suffer severe losses in a bond fund, just as you can with stocks.

As people run away from equities, some have been jumping into the next sinking boat and don't realize it. Let's say an investor owns a bond with a yield of 4 percent, and the prevailing market rate rises to 5 percent. There's less demand for that 4 percent bond now—investors want the higher rate. When demand falls, so does price, and if such bonds are the backbone of your portfolio, you are in trouble. If you need money at a time when rates have risen and bond prices have fallen, then you might have to sell at a loss. It's not a risk-free investment.

TAX ISSUES

Sometimes you can make more money by saving taxes than you can by making more money. This is important to understand, particularly considering what is inevitable: History reflects that taxes tend to rise.

We are in one of the lowest tax environments since the beginning of the last century. During 1944 and 1945, the top tax rate was at its all-time high of 94 percent, which was applied to incomes over $200,000[17]. The highest rate recently was in 1980, when the top tax bracket was 70 percent for incomes over $212,000.

It's important to understand the difference between taxable, tax-deferred and tax-free investing. Let's take a look at how each would affect a typical account. Suppose you started with $100,000 and added $10,000 each year for 20 years. Let's presume a rate of return of 4 percent and a tax bracket of 25 percent.

- ◆ On a tax-free account, the account value after 20 years would be $516,893.

- ◆ On a fully taxable account, your rate of return is effectively only 3 percent. After 20 years, the account value would be $449,315.

- ◆ On a tax-deferred account, your account value after 20 years would again be $516,893. However, you have only postponed taxes. If you now paid them all, you would be left with an account value of $462,670. Few people would do that, however; most would liquidate only part of the account, leaving the remainder to grow.

On its face, that appears to be a good-better-best scenario. It's good to save money, even when fully taxed. It's better to defer the taxes, and it's best to be free of the taxes. All this presumes that the tax brackets wouldn't change over those 20 years. If they increase—and they likely will—then it's questionable whether tax-deferred is truly better than taxable.

---

[17]Tax Foundation, "Federal Individual Income Tax Rates History: Income Years 1913-2011

This raises important issues for the millions of investors who have much of their life savings tied up in retirement plans such as 401(k)s and IRAs. The tax-deferment consequence, in fact, is such an important issue that I will devote a coming chapter to it.

An important mistake to avoid is this: paying taxes on money that you do not need for income and are just reinvesting. It's a common mistake and quite avoidable. For example, people earn a low rate on CDs and then pay taxes on those earnings, just to reinvest it all in another CD.

Here is some simple advice: You should only pay taxes on money you are withdrawing as money to spend. Otherwise, there may be better ways to manage it.

An option for a retiree may be a tax-deferred vehicle such as an annuity. You might wonder why that may be better than a tax-free vehicle such as a municipal bond. Here's why: If you make too much money, part of your Social Security income becomes taxable. Municipal bond income counts toward that threshold. Annuities do not, although your money may be subject to a surrender penalty for a period of time.

It's no small matter: Depending on how much you earn, 85 percent of your Social Security benefit can be subject to tax again[18]. You paid taxes all your working years so you could get the benefit, and now you find the benefit itself taxed.

To find out the Social Security tax consequence, first figure out your modified adjusted gross income, which is on your tax return. It includes pension, wages, interest and dividends, and even tax-exempt

---

[18]www.ssa.gov/pubs/EN-05-10035.pdf (April 2013)

interest such as that from municipal bonds. Then, figure how much half of your Social Security benefits are for the year – that's called your provisional income. The IRS allows a married couple filing jointly to have $32,000 in income. If it's between $32,000 - $44,000, up to 50 percent of the benefit is subject to tax. If the combined income exceeds $44,000, then up to 85 percent of the benefit is subject to tax. For singles, the thresholds are $25,000 and $34,000.

Most people don't know how to reduce that tax on their Social Security. They think that's just the way it is. But by taking some of your interest income—from those CDs, for example, or from municipal bonds—and putting that money into a deferred annuity, you perhaps could lower the tax on your Social Security from 85 percent down to 50 percent, or perhaps to zero. Over the years, that's a big impact on how much money you have in your pocket.

Tax-law is subject to frequent change; therefore it is important to coordinate with your tax advisor for the latest IRS rulings and specific tax advice concerning your particular situation. It's not uncommon for some people to have large amounts of money accumulated in tax-deferred accounts. The money is just sitting there, waiting to be taxed heavily upon death and inheritance. Meanwhile, these people may very well be in a zero marginal tax bracket because of a lot of medical expenses. It is quite possible that they could have about $15,000 more in interest income and still pay no taxes.

They have a CPA. Was that discussed? In my opinion, it's not the mindset of most tax preparers. They're great at calculating how much you owe. They can get to the bottom of a problem. They may do a wonderful job of preparing your return based on what you have done—but you may not hear much about what you should have done. In fact, you may not hear that from a lot of financial planners, either. They may just cross their arms and point to someone else. That's why you may need someone to coordinate your financial affairs and bring it all together.

FEES FOR PROBATE

In discussing fees, there's another kind that you must recognize for its potential to affect your bottom line, and that's the cost of probate in settling your estate. You will be reading more about estate planning later in this book, but for now let's take a look at those fees

The costs of probate are basically set by state law and may include appraisal costs, executor fees, court costs, the cost for a type of an insurance policy known as a surety bond, plus the legal and accounting fees.

Probate can easily cost from 3 to 7 percent of the estate value, or more. And if there is a contested will, then all bets are off. Probate costs are less in certain states where it is relatively simple, as compared with other states where it is expensive[19]. Tools such as living trusts can be valuable estate planning tools, but they are still sometimes oversold[20] because of people's fear of probate costs. Probate costs vary by state. Any tax or legal information provided here is merely a summary of our understanding and interpretation of some of the current regulations and is not exhaustive. Consult your legal or tax advisor for advice and information concerning your particular situation.

---

[19]USA-Probate.com - www.usa-probate.com/probate_faq.php#20 (2008)

[20]Four Facts of Living Trusts – Kiplinger (July 12,2014)

www.kiplinger.com/article/retirement/T021-C000-S001-four-facts-of-living-trusts.html

You hear stories in which probate has dragged on for decades, but for a typical family it may be a fairly simple process. Again, whether it is expensive and calls for attorneys will depend on the state. The state surrogate's office can provide details.

HEALTH-CARE AND LONG-TERM-CARE NEEDS

Will you get sick or become incapacitated during retirement? This is a major worry on the minds of many retirees, and for good reason: If you don't plan properly, the need for medical and long-term care has the potential to wipe away your nest egg.

"What's the point?" you may wonder. You may say, "Why not just spend my money now and enjoy it while I'm healthy, because everyone gets old and sick and it all disappears. That's just the way it works. There's nothing you can do."

Yes, it could be a huge risk, but there's always something you can do. The following chapter will take a close look at what that might be.

{ CHAPTER SEVEN }

Worried Sick

When I was a child, my grandparents lived with us. My mother didn't work outside the home very much, but she worked very hard within it, and a lot of that eventually entailed taking care of her parents.

For a modern-day family, that can cause a lot of emotional stress. It's a totally different scenario than the 1950s and '60s. Today, both spouses often work, and they may need every penny of both incomes. Their parents may live out West, their children may live down South—and nobody in the family is within driving distance, much less on the same street or in the same neighborhood. When someone in the family needs care, it couldn't be tougher to reach out.

The June 2011, Met Life study of Caregiving Costs to Working Caregivers found that a person's life expectancy actually could be significantly reduced by going through that caregiver experience. The caregiver may also suffer a substantial loss of wages, retirement benefits, and 401(k) contributions and matches.

When new clients bring up the subject of long-term care, it is most likely because something has awakened them to the need, sort of like the way people look into buying life insurance: "Joe next door just died of a heart attack—we'd better get another $250,000 of coverage, honey."

A lot of people don't think about how they will pay for long-term care needs until it is too late—the cost has gone up and benefits have been adjusted. You likely don't save money by waiting.

When you are buying insurance for pennies on the dollar of what you would pay for the care out of pocket, the cost of the insurance may not be the problem, but rather may be a solution to the problem. In New Jersey, the annual cost of long-term care exceeds $109,000 (State-Specific Data from Genworth 2012 Cost of Care Survey).

AN UNDERESTIMATED NEED

The costs of medical and long-term care are often underestimated, and some retirees do not even consider them—and yet they are one of the primary reasons that people run short of money in retirement.

"A lot of people don't have very good information about what their expenses will be in retirement," says Olivia S. Mitchell[21], professor of insurance and risk management at Wharton University. The Pension Research Council has found that people substantially minimize their need for long-term and nursing home insurance.

According to a May 7, 2012 survey, conducted by Harris Interactive for Nationwide Financial, nearly half of high-net-worth Americans who are close to retirement are "terrified" of what health-care costs could do to their retirement plans. But 38 percent of those surveyed said that they haven't discussed retirement health-care costs with a financial advisor, in part because they are unsure as to whether

---

[21]"How Much Money Will You Need for Retirement? More Than You Think." Aug 27, 2003

their advisor is knowledgeable about the issue. This is not a good sign.

It is important for financial advisors to spend time with clients identifying and projecting the health care costs they are likely to face. By reviewing their personal and family health history, an assessment of future out-of-pocket costs could be done and built those into their financial plan.

People don't understand what medical costs may be in retirement, and they often fail to see the risks posed by inflation. And I think they grossly underestimate their need for long-term care. It comes down to this: Several years of care can wipe out half a million dollars of life savings. What will be left for the surviving spouse?

"Well, it's not going to happen to me," you may think, but statistically, it will. The lifetime chance that someone who buys a policy at age 60 will use their policy before they die is 50 percent. A more responsible approach is to analyze the cost and look for ways to fund it[22].

People may think they will need to pay for the cost of insurance out of their cash flow—and as a result they worry that they won't be able to go out to dinner or visit the grandkids or play a round of golf. But often they do have money, perhaps half a million or so, so the fact that they have assets is what raises the issue. If they had no money, then Medicaid would be their plan.

In effect, then, the real problem is the fact that they have money— and my philosophy is that if the money is the problem, then let the

---

[22]Long term care probability or the risk you'll need long term insurance.

money pay for the problem. For example, if you have half a million in CDs or some other highly conservative investment, you may be able to reposition that from your left pocket to your right pocket. Even with a bond type of yield, you may be able to get enough additional income to pay for the long-term-care insurance.

There are different ways of funding the problem. It does not have to come out of cash flow.

THE SOONER THE BETTER

The 2012 Long-Term-Care Insurance Sourcebook published by The American Association of Long-Term Care Insurance has statistics on the percentage of applicants who are declined. From age 50 to 59, 16 percent are declined; from 60 to 69, it's 24 percent; from 70 to 79, it's 41 percent; and for ages 80 and over, it's 63 percent[23].

They also lose good health discounts as they get older. From age 50 to 59, 32 percent get a good health discount. From age 70 to 79, only 17 percent get one.

Why do some people get declined and lose the discounts? Not because they wait too long in and of itself, but because they wait too long and their health changes for the worse. They may be hoping to save money, but instead end up paying more because the insurance cost rises as they get older, and the amount needed also rises due to inflation. It may not make sense to wait; the statistics show that you are likely to end up paying more. It's a mathematical fact.

Let's look at a hypothetical example. You are age 55. You want what we term a "standard" plan of coverage.

[23]When is the Best Time to Buy Long-Term Care Insurance? - www.lifesprk.com/seek-on/best-time-to-buy-long-term-care-insurance#sthash.9ffYDhmM.dpuf (2012)

That equals $172,600 in current benefits (based on a 4500 monthly benefit for a 3-year plan). Your cost is $1,057 per year because you qualify for the preferred health discount (spousal discount too).

Long-term-care insurance protection should grow to keep pace with rising costs. The one we are illustrating does. So, by age 65, the $172,600 benefit you bought at age 55 will have grown in benefit value to $211,374 at a 3 percent compound inflation.

Someone age 65 (today) would pay $2,543 for $211,374 in coverage because it's very unlikely they will still qualify for that good health discount.

And that reflects today's rates. Chances are rates will rise. So, the 55 year old who waits for the 10 years will pay even more.

It almost never pays to wait. And, there is one more important point. While you are waiting, you are uninsured. If something happens causing you to need long-term care (such as an accident or an illness), you'll have to pay yourself. And, while most people need long-term care in their 70s and 80s, some do need care in their 50s and 60s.

WHAT ABOUT MEDICARE AND MEDICAID?

Some people still are thinking, "Well, I'll just depend on Medicare and maybe Medicaid." They don't realize how limited Medicare is in covering any type of benefits like that. To get any coverage for a nursing facility, you have to be in the hospital for at least three days, then be discharged and admitted to the facility within 30 days for the same condition. If you can jump through those hoops of fire, then you can get 100 days of coverage, for which you will still pay 20 percent. And after that, it's done.

Not many people qualify for even that limited amount of coverage[24]. The government has made it explicitly clear that it doesn't pay for long-term care—it's clear in brochures and other publications—so people should get the message that Medicare is not their solution for long-term care. Medicare should be viewed like health insurance.

The use of Medicaid to provide care has also been greatly restricted. The policies are clear: Medicaid is not to be used as a solution for wealthy people to transfer their money and save it. Medicaid was created for the purpose of providing medical assistance to low-income Americans. Some people feel too proud to go on Medicaid, even though they lack assets and can't afford long-term care insurance. Meanwhile, some wealthy people are trying to get on those rolls. They try to reposition their assets to make themselves indigent on paper—but it's much harder to accomplish that than it was 10 or 15 years ago.

Think about it: If you have half a million dollars and are feeling all right, are you going to give it all away to your children and grandchildren because you are worried that you might get sick? No reasonable person is going to do that.

THE COW AND THE MILK

Years ago, a farmer and I were discussing long-term care insurance. He was having trouble grasping why he needed it and how he could pay for it.

---

[24]Who Pays for a Nursing Home? www.life.familyeducation.com (8/10/2014)

"Let me ask you something," I said. "I'm looking out at your fields. I see all your cows . . . "

"Yes, that's everything I own," he said.

"And out in that field is a rat hole somewhere, I'd assume; would that be correct?"

"Yep, that'd be correct," he said.

"Then let's consider the nursing home, a rat hole. Is that ok with you?"

"Yep, that sounds about right," he laughed.

"Well, if you get sick and need to go into a nursing home," I said, "you might have to sell off a fifth of your herd every year for five years until they're all gone—or else you can set aside some of the milk now from some of the cows so that you can protect the whole herd."

"OK," he said. "I get it. You just want me to take a little bit of interest off some of my CDs and buy long-term care insurance so I don't lose it all."

He finally understood what I had been trying to tell him. He would be better off giving up some of the milk, or else he'd be risking the whole herd.

MEDICAID SPEND-DOWN REQUIREMENTS

The specifics on how much of one's assets must be spent before qualifying for Medicaid benefits varies by state. Simply stated, the spend-down is the process of depleting money until the appropriate asset level is reached.

A recent asset limit in the state of New Jersey is $2,000 for the Medicaid-only program and $4,000 for the medically needy program[25]. Different rules apply for married couples than apply to individuals. To qualify for Medicaid as an individual, you have to be at least 65 years old and have limited income--$1,800 a month or less for the Medicaid-only program or more than $1,800 a month for the medically needy program—and be otherwise incapable of paying for medical care.

If you have a medical need and anticipate entering a nursing home or assisted living facility, I recommend that you contact an elder-law attorney who specializes in such issues. Spending down to qualify for Medicaid is much more difficult than it once was, but such attorneys can be a godsend in helping people protect some of their money and in getting the type of care they otherwise might not be able to obtain.

The amount of the spend-down is determined based on the assets of the couple as of the day the institutionalized spouse enters the facility, hospital, home or assisted living facility for an extended stay. This date is referred to as the "snapshot date" by Medicaid. There are various exemptions and allowances that are available to couples that

---

[25]New Jersey Medicaid Moving Forward in 2014, Medicaid.gov

www.medicaid.gov/Medicaid-CHIP-Program-Information/By-State/new-jersey.html

aren't available to single individuals. The family home is exempt from spend-down, as is the family car.

The community spouse, the one who is still living at home, is entitled to a community spouse resource allowance. They're also allowed a minimum monthly maintenance allowance. A single individual is not entitled to any allowances other than $35 a month for personal needs. The allowances for the community spouse are intended to protect the community spouse from being pauperized, but it's still very limited. We refer couples to a website that we created called www.SaveTheSpouse.com for a report.

The process of disposing of assets in order to qualify for Medicaid has become tougher because of an extended look-back period, which is how far back the government examines your finances. It used to be three years; now, it's five. One strategy that some people can use is to buy a long-term-care policy with a five-year benefit period. If they need care during that time, the policy pays for it for five years while they immediately begin transferring assets, with the help of an elder-law attorney.

If you live in a partnership state such as New Jersey[26], consider this: If you buy, for example, a policy with a benefit of $200 a day for five years, or $365,000 total, and you use up that benefit, you can then set aside that same amount of money over and above the Medicaid limits. You can keep that money and still qualify for Medicaid. It allows you to preserve a substantial amount of wealth. Long-term-care insurance is smart. People just don't understand all the nuances of what they can do or should do.

---

[26]Feb 12, 2008 - New Jersey Long-Term Care Insurance Partnership Program

www.state.nj.us/dobi/bulletins/blt08_08.pdf

VETERAN BENEFITS

Aid and Attendance for Veterans is also a helpful program for those who qualify. U.S. wartime veterans and surviving spouses may be able to receive assistance to help with the cost of assisted living care, depending on income level.

The benefit, however, likely will not be enough to pay for that care. For 2013[27], the maximum annual benefit for a veteran with no spouse or dependent children is $20,784. If the veteran is married and requires care, the maximum is $24,648; the maximum for a surviving spouse is $13,356. If you qualify for this benefit, you should apply for it but it is not an alternative to long-term-care insurance. Think of it as a supplement that could reduce the amount of insurance you need.

ALTERNATIVE PRODUCTS

Even though the odds of needing long-term care are, basically, 50/50, same as the flip of a coin, most people consider themselves to be in the half who will not need it. People picture themselves younger and healthier and better looking than they are. It's human nature. But the truth is that you or your spouse stand a good chance of needing such care, and one way or another you need to plan for it.

"Well, I've got this $300,000 in a CD," you might be thinking. "We'll leave it in the bank and we'll just use that. That should be enough to pay for care." And that's one approach, but is there a better one? Some products have come out that are not really substitutes but

---

[27] 2010 American Veterans Aid, info@americanveteransaid.com

alternatives. There are products out there that provide a long-term care benefit linked to a single premium life insurance policy.

Let's say you took out a $150,000 policy and at about age 65 you may get double that in a death benefit right off the bat. If you need long-term care, you can access that money for a monthly benefit that is tax free.

Therefore, you may not need to be parking money in low-yielding CDs. You can often get a higher rate of return in these contracts, and with some you can change your mind in the early years and get 100 percent of your money back.

ASSET-BASED LTC INSURANCE

This is a popular hybrid of life insurance and long-term-care insurance that is underwritten for both mortality and morbidity. It is much like self-insuring but provides substantially more leverage per dollar. For example, a 60-year-old woman in good health can invest $100,000 into this type of policy and receive an initial death benefit of $265,000 with a LTC benefit of $436,000. This would give her five years of coverage at up to $6,057 per month. The insurance company accelerates the death benefit to provide tax-free monthly long-term-care benefits. This example includes a simple interest inflation adjustment of 3 percent annually. The client can take back her full $100,000 investment at any time for 15 years with no penalty.

Asset-based LTC insurance is ideal for high-net-worth individuals who would otherwise self-insure or who have money in a CD or other under-performing investment. This type of plan creates a tremendous opportunity to maximize your return on investment. By transferring the money to the insurance company, the company is "on the hook" for life insurance and long-term-care protection without jeopardizing access to the funds if they are needed for something else.

The Pension Protection Act of 2006 created an opportunity for annuity owners to use their non-qualified annuity—meaning it's not an IRA—to pay their qualified long-term-care insurance premiums tax-free. Effective as of 2010, the Internal Revenue Code Section 1035 was expanded under the act to allow tax-free exchanges from annuity and life insurance contracts to qualified long-term-care contracts.

That makes it possible to surrender an existing annuity or a life insurance contract, which is generally taxable as income, to the extent of the gain in the contract. When that annuity or life-insurance contract is exchanged for another, the transfer is nontaxable. That allows another opportunity for people to possibly avoid taxes so that they can help fund long-term care.

Today you can get life insurance policies with a terminal illness provision. For example, if you have less than six months or a year to live, you will be allowed to access a high percentage—say, 94 percent—of the death benefit while you are living[28]. Why would you want to do that? Maybe you never saw the Eiffel Tower or you want to take the grandkids to Hawaii for your last trip. Perhaps you want to pay for medical treatment in Mexico that your HMO doesn't cover. I know people who have done that; they want to hold on to hope.

Or, you can use a life insurance policy to pay for long-term care. Surrender charges in contracts such as annuities often are waived

---

[28]All guarantees are based on the claims paying ability of the issuer.

for a long-term-care event. There are annuities that provide guaranteed income for a lifetime that will double that amount if you need long-term care.

As an example, a well-known insurance company has an annuity policy in which an individual can withdraw income at a 6 percent annual rate. If she elects to take 6 percent or less, the income is guaranteed for life. If she's in a nursing home, the income doubles to a 12 percent annual rate for life, even if the money runs out. At a similar 12 percent withdrawal rate, the money would be about gone in eight years, but the payments in the contract continue even beyond those eight years. Only an insurance company can guarantee that.

There are many things you can do to protect yourself, beyond just using your own money to pay for long-term care. I use an acronym called OPM—other people's money. You should always try to use other people's money to do things rather than your own. There are alternatives. Through good planning with an elder care lawyer and a financial advisor, you don't need to be worried sick.

CHAPTER EIGHT

The 401(k) Fallacy

B ack in 1978, Congress added a section to the Internal Revenue Code that was intended to offer taxpayers a break on deferred income[29]. It was an obscure provision, but two years later, benefits consultant Ted Benna, co-owner of the Johnson Cos., was redesigning the retirement program for Philadelphia-based Cheltenham National Bank when he realized that the provision allowed employers to use salary deductions as tax-deferred contributions to employee retirement plans. He soon created and gained IRS approval of the first 401(k) savings plan, allowing the use of employee salary deductions as a source of retirement contributions.

These retirement plans yielded a major crop of new investors, but many might not have been fully aware of the inherent risk within these plans. When Enron and WorldCom tanked in 2001 and 2002, employees who had invested large portions of their own 401(k) retirement contributions in the company stock experienced devastating losses.

For the most part, the 401(k) plans replaced pensions as the prevailing vehicle for people's retirement. But surveys and studies show

---

[29]A Brief History Of: The 401(k), Time Magazine, Oct. 16, 2008

some very bleak numbers. The balances in 401(k)s and IRAs may not be nearly enough to pay for comfortable retirements, as the previous generation's pensions once did. And today, few companies offer pensions—mostly, they only are for the public sector.

Why is it possible that 401(k)s and IRAs may not provide as much retirement income as a pension? There are several reasons. First, not all companies offer 401(k) plans, just as some companies did not offer pensions. However, investors who do contribute to 401(k) plans often are unaware of the array of annual charges, such as administration fees, sales charges, management fees, and individual services that they are paying and that are siphoning away their earnings. Fees aren't "hidden" so much as they're judiciously disclosed. Many people simply don't know how or where to look for those fees.

Most people are not sophisticated investors and pay little attention to those fees, and in addition, they have faced poor stock market returns since 2000. In 2012, new regulations required full fee disclosure.

THE BOTTOM LINE

Fees, regardless of how conspicuously they're disclosed, should be but one criterion you pick for your 401(k) investments. Look at asset class, management's relative competence, and track record first. Each of them will have a far greater impact on your long-term returns than fees.

INSUFFICIENT SAVING

Vanguard does a report every year called "How America Saves" on the 401(k)-type plans that it manages. The 2013 Vanguard report has some interesting insights: Thirty-two percent of employees do not contribute to a 401(k). Among employees ages 25 and younger, 59 percent do not contribute, and 27 percent of employees older than 55 do not contribute. Among employees with incomes greater than $100,000, 12 percent do not contribute. The median employee contribution rate is 6 percent, with 21 percent of employees contributing more than 10 percent. Nine percent of employees contribute the maximum allowed by law.

The Vanguard report said that, including any employer match, employees with an income of between $50,000 and $100,000 should save at least 12 percent of their income, and they should save at least 15 percent if their income is over $100,000.

When people ask us how much they should be saving, we tell them that ideally, if they want to retire with the same purchasing power in the future as they have today, they need to set aside a minimum of 15 percent. Under the old pension system, people contributed 15 to 20 percent. The companies built that amount into the benefit package when they put money into a pension plan; in other words, employees received less compensation because they had the pension.

Nothing stops people from saving at that rate today, but many may not be doing so. The picture there is pretty clear: If people don't contribute to their 401(k)s, or if they don't contribute enough, of course they are not going to have enough in their accounts to cover their retirement.

Nonetheless, for the last three decades, money has been primarily directed into these retirement accounts. At unprecedented levels, people are putting money aside, even though they are not doing as much as may be necessary and could be falling short of the amount required to retire comfortably. The 401(k)s and IRAs[30] have pretty much replaced pensions, but people may not have the investment skills needed to deal with them properly.

Because people often change employers, it's not unusual for them to have multiple accounts from previous jobs. Ordinarily, that would be a good thing since they've been able to start accumulating some wealth, but what we see is that when people change jobs, they tend to look at their account with the previous employee as found money.

They withdraw it and end up paying a penalty of 10 percent, if they are younger than age 59½. Not only that, but there will be taxes due on the contributions and earnings of the "windfall" which may also result in putting them into a higher tax bracket.

The result is that they may lose 40 percent of that money. If that's the way you save for retirement, you are always starting from zero. You simply might not have the money you'll need to make it if you waste 10, 15, or 20 years of savings just so you can get a condo at the beach or a new car.

ONE COMMON MISCONCEPTION

Since the inception of these deferred-tax plans, they have been portrayed to the working public as an ideal way to save for retirement. "You may be in a lower tax bracket then," the reasoning goes, "so you won't take as big a hit when you finally have to pay the IRS."

[30]Age, income and contribution limits vary for each plan.

Actually, that may not necessarily be the case. For one thing, your objective is to be successful and to make more money, and that likely will put you into a higher tax bracket. How would it be that you would be in a lower tax bracket—because your income fell? Who wants their income to be less in retirement? A lot of working families are living on 100 percent of their income, so how could they live on less after they stopped working? It's just not realistic.

And tax rates are probably not going to go down. They already are at a historic low, as I pointed out in Chapter 6. Consider the current state of the federal deficit, and you will see that tax rates will most likely be going up to fund that deficit. There simply is very little chance that the majority of people will find themselves in a lower tax bracket in the future.

Imagine that you are a farmer and the tax man pays a visit. He tells you that you have a choice: You can pay your taxes on the value of the seeds that you purchase in the spring before you plant your crops, or else you can pay your taxes on the value of the harvest in the fall, when you make all your money. I don't think anyone would hesitate to pay the taxes on the seeds.

You can think of your 401(k), traditional or Roth IRA contributions that way. Would it be smarter to pay the taxes up front on the "seeds?" You may want to explore options for investing in a tax-deferred environment. Come harvest time—that is, your retirement—you could then have some money that you can withdraw without further taxes. If you have been a good farmer, or investor, that's when you may have your most wealth. And don't be misled: That's also when you may be in a higher tax bracket. A bountiful crop alone could put you in a higher bracket, and the tax rate may rise.

As we will see later in this chapter, the seeds-versus-harvest question illustrates the fundamental difference between the traditional deferred-tax retirement plans and the Roth IRA plans in which you pay the tax up front: In other words, you may prefer to pay the tax on the seeds rather than the harvest.

As in most instances, there are basic advantages and disadvantages of Roth IRA accounts, as well as how they differ from traditional IRAs. The complexity of the tax laws covering traditional and Roth IRAs can make it difficult to decide between the two options. Consult with your tax adviser about the best way to make contributions to retirement accounts to maximize the tax benefits and your future financial security.

REQUIRED MINIMUM DISTRIBUTIONS

Years ago, the IRS used to levy what was known as an excess distributions and accumulation tax penalty on these retirement plans—a "Success Tax," if you will—an additional 15 percent tax[31] if you saved too much for your retirement. At least the government has done away with that. It does require you to begin withdrawing money from your account by April 1 of the year following the year in which you turn 70½. At that point, generally you have to open up the spigot whether or not you want and need the money. You have to take out money and pay taxes on it. Roth IRAs do not require distributions until after the death of the owner.

If you don't take a required minimum distribution, you may have to pay a 50 percent penalty on the amount not distributed as

[31]American Association of Individual Investors - www.aaii.com/journal/article/retirement-plan-rules-ira-options-proliferate-under-tax-law-changes (October 1997)

required, so it's not pleasant. The government is very serious about not leaving that money in retirement accounts too long. And as the account owner, you are the one who is responsible for calculating the amount of the required minimum distribution. You have to make sure that you are taking out the proper amount. It's not the institution's sole responsibility.

If you do not need the money in your retirement account, there is a strategy that could potentially increase your returns. Let's say that you have a $500,000 IRA and you turn 70½ and must start your withdrawals. The account could be split into two IRAs. Most of the money—let's say $400,000—could go into a new IRA with more growth-oriented products. The government says that you have to take a minimum withdrawal based on all your IRA money; however, it does not require you to take a proportionate amount on each account.

Why split your money into two accounts? You can use the smaller one for the withdrawals while allowing the other account to potentially grow unhindered, which may minimize any sequence of return risk on most of your money.

Sequence of returns risk involves the actual order in which investment returns occur. Typically, negative returns earlier in retirement have a more severe impact on your portfolio than negative returns later in retirement.

STRETCH PROVISIONS FOR YOUR HEIRS

The required distributions are designed so that theoretically, your distribution period is always greater than your age[32], presuming a

---

[32]IRS - www.irs.gov/pub/irs-tege/uniform_rmd_wksht.pdf (Revised 8/12/2014)

normal growth rate. So for many retirees, the money doesn't run out. There is money left for heirs. It's important to consider how that money is passed on.

The beneficiary of what is called "an inherited IRA" can opt to continue the tax-deferred growth; the rules for required distributions allow for such a "stretch" provision[33]. He or she can take distributions over a fixed period of time, based on life expectancy. For example, a 20-year-old beneficiary can take payments over 63 additional years. Special rules apply to spousal beneficiaries after that.

A word of caution, though: Given the choice of a lump sum or tax-deferred distribution (and I have seen this happen many times), most heirs seem to know only four words: "Show me the money." While you might appreciate the value of tax-deferred growth, your beneficiary might prefer instant gratification. He or she isn't thinking about tax consequences or investing for the future. Instead, a shiny new car beckons. You may have been thinking Cornell, but they're thinking Corvette.

If that's the case, then there's very little to prevent your beneficiary from simply taking a lump sum distribution upon inheriting the IRA rather than stretching those distributions out over his or her life expectancy.

It's possible, though, to name a trust as the beneficiary of your IRA to establish some control over how distributions will be taken after your death. I think of this as "ruling from the grave."

Some people have set up a trust for only one child in the family because they considered that child to not be good at managing

---

[33]Investopedia - www.investopedia.com/terms/s/stretch-ira.asp (Revised 8/12/2014)

money. "My son and one of my daughters are fine with it," one man said, "but the other daughter, she's dancing over in Russia and she'd be drinking vodka with the Russian ballet. It'd all be gone."

You have to consider whether family situations call for such action. With a stretch IRA, the distributions could potentially be spread over three generations. The money could be in deferral for a long time. A starting balance of $500,000 could result in total payments of over $2 million to multiple generations.

One little caveat here is on spousal planning on these stretches: IRA owners should understand that IRA money left to a spouse comes under the control of that spouse, giving him or her the power to do anything that the IRA rules allow. The surviving spouse has the power to include or exclude heirs. If you have children from a first marriage, for example, your surviving spouse can cut them out in a heartbeat once she gets that money. If you suspect that might happen, you may want to consider having multiple beneficiaries or setting up a trust. That way you maintain control even from beyond the grave.

Most heirs will not know that a stretch is available to them—and if they do, they could fail to get the full benefit from it, or they could be tempted to take the lump sum. IRA owners can do themselves and their heirs a big favor by setting this up in advance, in some way, shape, or fashion. They could reach out to the heirs, while the account owner is still alive, and explain the distributions available to them and to whom they can go to for guidance when the time comes for distribution.

CONVERTING TO A ROTH

You may find it advantageous to convert your traditional IRA to a Roth IRA, in which the taxes are paid up front and the eventual distribution comes to you tax free.

Converting is not that big of an issue, technically. It can be a big issue financially, however, because you face the prospect of paying those taxes in the year of conversion. Above all, however, the conversion has to make sense.

Consider this: If you don't plan to spend the money in your lifetime but instead will be leaving it to heirs as legacy money, who really should be paying the taxes? Do you want to convert to a Roth and pay the taxes yourself if they are just likely to take a lump sum and spend it? That could be a likely scenario unless you put the money into a trust.

For a married couple who want to convert to a Roth but who do not have the money to pay the taxes, one strategy may be to purchase a life insurance policy that we can use is a spousal Roth conversion. Let's say the husband and wife are both living, it's the husband's IRA account, and the couple does not need the money in the account. When it comes time to take the required minimum distributions, one option may be to purchase a life insurance policy on the husband in the amount projected to be necessary to pay the taxes upon his death so that his wife can convert the account to a tax-free Roth.

Let's say that it would require $100,000 in taxes to convert a $400,000 account. When the husband dies, the wife inherits the $400,000, and she also receives a $100,000 death benefit. She could use the life insurance money to pay the taxes, and now she has a

$400,000 Roth. That's a way to accomplish a conversion without having to come up with the money right away.

This strategy may not be advantageous for many as finding affordable life insurance can be a difficult task; most life insurance policies require health underwriting and, in some cases, financial underwriting, and the cost of premiums may be more than the potential taxes.

It may not be the wisest decision to pay the conversion taxes from the Roth itself as it could take years to replenish those dollars. In the wild, it's called eating your young. You don't want to do that, so it may really only make sense if you can use money from another account.

Any discussion of tax rules included in or related to this article is for general informational purposes only. Such discussion does not purport to be complete or to cover every situation. Consult a qualified professional for tax advice specific to your situation.

THE BACKDOOR ROTH

You can get what is known as a "backdoor Roth" by opening up what's called a non-deductible IRA now and then converting it to a Roth. In 2014 you can contribute $5,500 a year or $6,500 if you're 50 or older.

Why would you do that? The issue is that people with high incomes cannot open a Roth IRA directly. Since 2010, however, Congress has allowed Roth conversions[34] for all taxpayers regardless of their income. High-income earners can get a Roth by doing this two-step process.

[34]IRA FAQs - Rollovers and Roth Conversions - http://www.irs.gov/Retirement-Plans/Retirement-Plans-FAQs-regarding-IRAs-Rollovers-and-Roth-Conversions (4/11/2014)

One caveat that comes up is what is called a "pro rata rule," and that means that you have to aggregate all of your IRAs to determine how much income tax you owe when you convert. If you have no other IRAs and you open a $5,000 non-deductible IRA and then convert it, you only owe taxes on the earnings, if any.

By contrast, if you have a $95,000 traditional IRA in pre-tax contributions and you convert a $5,000 non-deductible contribution to a new IRA, the conversion would be 95 percent taxable. So how do you get around that? You transfer it to a 401(k). Many employers allow roll-ins of IRA money to their 401(k)s.

If you are self-employed with no employees other than perhaps your spouse, you could establish an individual 401(k), roll over your IRA money into the plan, and then do it that way. There are many other advantages for a small business in establishing an individual 401(k), such as possible higher contribution limits and loan provisions.

The lesson once again is that there often are ways to accomplish what you might have felt was impossible. A typical retiree won't know about these, and as a result could take an unnecessary blow to his or her nest egg or legacy. You need to work in concert with an advisor who can help point the way to a prosperous future for you and your loved ones.

{ CHAPTER NINE }

Footprints for Posterity

Several years ago, two couples came to my office during the same week. One had about $600,000, and they were looking to just get a reasonable rate of return on the money. They didn't need much for themselves. They were very frugal. It was important to them that their children would get a legacy. That's what their own parents had taught them was important. They wanted to help out the kids later on.

Later in the week, another couple came in, and they also had about $600,000. They wanted to be spending their last dollar as they took their last breath. I believe that they had a bumper sticker on their car that said: "We're spending our children's inheritance." It wasn't important to them that the kids got anything. "We fed them, we changed their diapers, we educated them, and this is our time now. It's our money. We gave them everything, and they're on their own."

People have different goals about what will become of the money that they spent decades accumulating. They want to live comfortably. Whether they want anything left over to help others live comfortably is another matter.

A good financial advisor will find out right away what those expectations are. Your goals and expectations have everything to do with how your financial plan must be devised. Some financial planners will pronounce a solution for handling prospective clients' money as soon as they see it—without knowing the objectives. And as you can see, those objectives can be as diverse as "everything to the kids" and "nothing to the kids." Without getting to know the client's purposes, recommendations may not be in line with their financial goals.

It's not that it's impossible to maintain your own lifestyle while leaving a nice inheritance. You don't necessarily have to choose one or the other. There are various financial vehicles that may be utilized to help you pursue the standard of living that you always anticipated while also leaving a legacy.

You must, however, come to terms with the balance that you feel is appropriate. In general, the more you spend on yourself, the less that will remain for your heirs. Imagine a scale. On one side is your lifestyle. On the other is a big legacy for your heirs. When one side tips down, the other rises.

Many advisors assume that people want to leave a lot of money to their kids, and more often than not they are correct. But frankly, not everybody wants to do that—or if they do, they find that they cannot.

In estimating how much they might be able to leave to heirs, people tend to make two major mistakes: They may underestimate inflation, and they could quite possibly underestimate their life expectancy. They may well end up with nothing left at all, even for themselves.

If you do have surplus money, it may come down to this: Are you willing to not enjoy that surplus and possibly reduce your standard of living so that you can leave a big legacy? Do you want to leave something for the kids or not? Or do you want to leave money for charity? Charitable giving is another issue that I will address in this chapter: How do you do it in a way that makes sense from a tax perspective?

To get a handle on what you truly want and what is possible, you may need to work with a professional who can design a plan. You need to thoroughly understand how the threats that I have described in this book (sequence of return risk, inflation, living too long, as just a few examples) apply to your unique situation. Online calculators may not be sufficient; they don't see you as human. If you input your numbers into three of them, they'll crunch them three different ways, none of which recognizes you, your goals, or your heart.

You have to weigh the quality of your relationships, as well. To whom do you want to leave money, and who must not get a cent? You may feel a need to protect your life savings from people who might not have your best interests in mind – some call this dealing with the "in-laws and the outlaws" and the "creditors and predators."

FEDERAL AND STATE TAX ISSUES

As of this writing, a change to the federal estate tax may affect fewer Americans. For 2014, decedents[35] with estates in excess of $5,340,000 million will be subject to the tax. The exemption amount is indexed for inflation each year. That's a dramatic change from the sunset provision that was in effect which would have lowered that amount to $1,000,000.

[35] Estate Tax – Internal Revenue Service - www.irs.gov/Businesses/Small-Businesses-&-Self-Employed/Estate-Tax (7/2/2014)

And remember that estates over the exemption amount are subject to a flat 40 percent tax rate.

"I don't have a problem," people tell me all the time, believing they will remain well within the exemption, but often they do not truly know the extent of what an estate entails. It takes into account the value of their home, their 401(k)s and life insurance. People underestimate life insurance. If they have a $5,340,000 million life insurance policy, they would already be at the limit for exemption, never mind the value of the house or retirement account or savings or anything else in the estate.

"I thought life insurance was tax free," people say, and it's true that it is free of income tax. But upon death, a life insurance policy translates from a piece of paper and a few drops of ink into a pile of cash—and a pile of cash is an estate asset, and it is taxable. People often misunderstand that.

Estate taxes on the state level are another issue. A few years ago, the feds were talking as if they were going to abolish the federal estate tax. A number of states decided that they would "decouple" and establish their own estate taxes. This happened because the federal government cut the states out: The previous practice had been that the feds would collect the entire tax and that a portion of the money collected in estate tax, a "soak up tax," would go to the states. The federal government never proceeded to abolish the tax, but the very prospect stirred many states, such as New Jersey, to enact their own subsequently larger tax.

As a result, what had seemed to be a tax that was going away instead got bigger for some. Most states don't have an estate tax, and for those that do, the rate varies. At the time of this writing, New Jersey does, and the state exemption is $675,000.

Just about everybody who has life insurance, a 401(k), and a house exceeds that limit, and people are shocked to find out that they have to pay an estate tax to two entities. Some states also have an inheritance tax, so depending on the state and their tax laws your estate could be subject to different taxes. For many people, the issue becomes not what they make, but what they can keep.

The information contained herein is based on current tax laws, which may change at any time and without notice. Each taxpayer should seek independent advice from a tax professional based on their particular situation

GETTING YOUR DOCUMENTS IN ORDER

I am amazed at how many successful people, and those who have children, do not have a will. They are almost embarrassed to tell me. I can understand why they would feel sheepish.

A will is a document by which a person can direct the distribution of assets when he or she dies. It is used to carry out the intention of the deceased as to who gets what. A will has many benefits. In general, it ensures that the assets are distributed according to your wishes when you die, and while you are alive it may give you a sense of comfort knowing your wishes will be carried out, or you have taken steps to put your affairs in order.

If you die without a will, the state steps in and distributes your assets according to the provisions of the state. It's called "dying intestate." In other words, everyone dies with a will—either the one that the state provides for you, or the one that you write to supersede it.

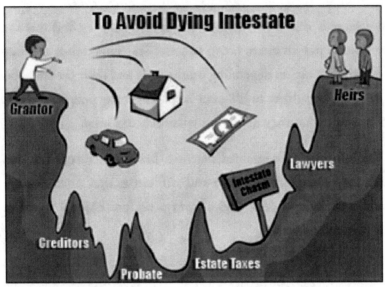

Courtesy of: M. Don Forbush, Certified Estate Advisor

You also may decide to set up a trust, or you could have a trust as part of a will. That is called a "testamentary trust," and it can come into play when you die to determine how money will be distributed over periods of time; for example, to young children as they reach a particular age.

You might also consider a living trust, which spells out your assets and your wishes for distributing them; it functions like a will except that its provisions are also in effect before you die. A living trust avoids probate, but you may really only need one if you live in a state where probate is complicated and expensive or you have property in multiple states or desire the secrecy of a trust.

A few additional legal papers that everyone should have include the following, which most attorneys now provide as part of an all-inclusive suite of documents:

♦ A living will, which you can think of as your right-to-die statement. It states your health-care directives regarding life-prolonging medical treatment. If the time comes when you no longer can speak for yourself, a living will directs your family and physicians on the actions they are to take.

♦ A health-care power of attorney, and a durable power of attorney—and these powers may be designated to different people. You may prefer that one person make decisions on the handling of your medical concerns, and you may want somebody else to have the durable power of attorney to look after your financial affairs or conduct other business for you if you become incapacitated.

WHO SHOULD HAVE A TRUST?

In some situations a trust may have a number of advantages over a will. With a trust, you can put conditions on how and when your assets will be distributed after you die. In general, you can use different kinds of trusts to reduce estate and gift taxes. It is an official way to distribute assets to heirs without the cost, delay, and publicity of probate.

If you establish your trust in states with more favorable creditor protection laws, you may be able to better protect your assets in the trust from creditors and from lawsuits. You can name a successor trustee who not only manages your trust after you die but is empowered to manage the trust assets if you become unable to do so.

Who should have one? Anybody who has a sizable amount of assets in real estate, a business, or even, say, an art collection should have a trust. It's a valuable document if you want to leave your estate to your heirs in a way that is not directly and immediately payable to them upon your death—such as to that Russian ballet dancer whom I mentioned earlier. You could set up a trust if you want to support a surviving spouse but also want to ensure that the principal or remainder of your estate goes to your chosen heirs—for example, your children from a first marriage—after your spouse dies. A trust also can allow you to provide for, say, a disabled child without disqualifying that child from Medicaid or other government assistance.

Setting up a trust will cost you several thousand dollars or possibly more depending on the complexity of the trust and your geographic location. It could be a small investment for a huge benefit way down the line. Trusts are also an extremely valuable tool when combined with life insurance policies.

Dividing your assets equally among heirs can be difficult. Deciding what and how much to leave will be two of your main considerations as you develop your estate plan. For example, leaving certain assets, such as a residence, to more than one heir can create administrative and practical challenges for the multiple owners. Similar difficulties can occur with a family business, especially if some heirs are more active in running the business than others. On the other hand, leaving a single asset entirely to one heir could create inequality unless your estate has sufficient liquidity to balance inheritances. In circumstances like these, to maintain good relations, liquidating the asset and distributing the proceeds often seem like the only option.

Consider life insurance as a possible solution. A life insurance death benefit can provide the liquidity that may be needed to give each heir the inheritance you want them to receive. You (or your trust) would purchase a life insurance policy on your life. The death benefit proceeds can be used to help provide heirs with inheritances of given projected values when assets are eventually distributed, helping to balance out the value of the "hard-to-divide" asset.

Information provided is intended for general informational and educational purposes only and is not intended to provide legal, tax or investment advice. Such discussion does not purport to be complete or to cover every situation. You are encouraged to consult with the appropriate professional in regard to your particular

CHARITABLE GIVING

Charities need legacy contributions. I have a saying: "What do you call a charity that doesn't have an endowment program?" and the answer is "extinct." Charities need to get those contributions in now, but they also need to have those large endowments coming in later.

There basically are four categories of charitable giving that we use. Two are simple methods and two are complex. The first of the simple methods is an outright gift. This may be appropriate for donors who want to see their charitable dollars at work during their lifetime.

Another is a bequest through the will. That's the basic method for those who want to give at the end of their life. Maybe they want to keep the money for themselves for now, and if they don't need it, it will go to a charity. Life insurance policies are used a lot to leverage a current gift for later. It may be possible for someone who is giving $5,000 a year to a charity to leverage that gift by purchasing a life insurance policy, whereby they could leave a death benefit of $100,000 or more later.

One of the complex methods involves what is known as life income gifts and split interest instruments. An example of those would include what are called a charitable gift annuity, which involves a contract between a donor and a charity, whereby the donor transfers cash or property to the charity in exchange for a partial tax deduction and a lifetime stream of annual income from the charity. When the donor dies, the charity keeps the gift.

The amount of the income stream is determined by many factors including the donor's age and the policy of the charity. Most charities use payout rates defined by the American Council on Gift Annuities. A charitable remainder trust is an irrevocable tax-exempt trust designed to transfer highly appreciated assets to a charity and retain a right to an income stream for non-charitable beneficiaries of the trust for a specified period of time; and then donating the remainder of the trust to the designated charity. A charitable lead trust is similar but works in reverse by donating a portion of the trust's income to charities and then, after a specified period of time, transferring the remainder of the trust to non-charitable beneficiaries. Another option is the pooled income fund, which is similar to a mutual fund created by a charity. The fund is comprised of irrevocable gifts that are pooled and invested together. Income from the fund is distributed to the fund's participants and other income beneficiaries (if named) according to their share of the fund. Upon the death of the donor and any other income beneficiaries, the value of the assets will be transferred to the charity.

Those are methods that may be appropriate for donors who want to give assets now for later use and who seek some form of direct financial return from their giving and who have unique tax and estate issues to deal with.

The other complex method is the establishing of a family foundation. This approach may be suitable for donors who want to keep their gifted capital intact while making smaller annual charitable distributions and retaining administrative control.

A BEQUEST FOR THE TAX MAN

Alternatively, you could do nothing to plan for charitable giving—and the money that could have gone to a cherished cause or institution may instead go to the government. In my opinion, that's a way of contributing to the public welfare, indeed, though it might not be the way you would like. You lose control.

There are three places where your money can go: to your family, to charity, or to the government. Pick two (Hint: most would pick family and charity). And if you don't make a choice, the government will be one of them by default.

Here in New Jersey, a major highway is Route 295. "You have a choice," I tell clients. "You can have your money take care of orphans and abused animals—or you can have it help to build an on-ramp to 295. It's up to you."

LEGACY PLANNING

My father fought in the Battle of the Bulge, and when I was a young boy I heard a lot of his war stories. They really got me interested in history and the world wars, particularly World War II.

When both of us knew that he had a limited time to live, I asked him to get deep and narrow with my two boys about his experiences so that they could have a personal and intimate understanding of their grandfather and what he had endured. They are in their mid- to late-20s now, and they are enthralled with history and virtually anything that has to do with the Second World War. Their grandfather left them a lasting legacy. He is forever vivid in their minds.

How many people know anything about their great grandparents or their great, great grandparents? It's as if memories fade to oblivion after a few generations. In legacy planning, we tell people there comes a time in life when you long to know that you had some purpose. You want to know that you are leaving a meaningful mark in the world. Done properly, legacy planning can help you use the resources and experience that you have accumulated in life to make a lasting impression on those you love and the causes you believe in.

It goes beyond wills and estate planning. Creating a legacy plan starts with a "bucket list" of the lifetime achievements that you desire, and it helps you to express your values and interests—what truly matters to you. You can document the essence of your life as a priceless bequest to your survivors.

Your legacy plan gives your loved ones clarity about which causes you believe in so that they can continue to support them. In that way, you can make an imprint. We ask clients two fundamental questions to get to the heart of the matter: "What will you leave behind?" and "How will you be remembered?"

Ernest Becker, the Pulitzer Prize-winning psychologist and author of The Denial of Death wrote, "What a man really fears is not so much extinction but extinction with insignificance." "Man wants to know that his life has somehow counted, if not for himself, then at least for a larger scheme of things, that it has left a trace, a trace that has meaning. Its effects must remain alive in eternity in some way."

{ CONCLUSION }

Safe Travels

F inancial security alone cannot define happiness. It doesn't bring you good health, a happy marriage and relationships, goodwill, or a sense of purpose. You first need to find a balance of all those and more in your life. After you identify the people and things you find important, you then can allocate your resources appropriately among them. That's what brings quality of life—not merely having money.

Money, however, helps.

We each define quality of life in our own way. We each have unique goals and dreams. Economic security can buy you time to focus your attention on what matters. My goal for you is to help you understand your own definition of the good life, and then work to make your money a tool toward achieving it.

In my opinion, you need to match your assets to your aspirations; in other words, you need to plan your life and legacy so that your life savings have meaning. Your spending should support your values and priorities. Otherwise, you may be blowing through money aimlessly, or you are just trying to grow your pile bigger. If making money is your sole pursuit, you are likely to take too many risks—and as you head into retirement, you are entering a territory where those risks can prove fatal to your portfolio.

As I have shared in these pages, I think of our journey from youth to maturity as a travel through two lands. The first I call Accumulation Land, when we are out seeking our fortune—both what we want to do in life, and the resources we will need to see us through. The second I call Distribution Land, when we look forward to eating the fruit of our hard work.

I hope by now you understand clearly that dangers prowl in Distribution Land. This is the one essential lesson that I want you to remember from this book: If you use the same investment and tax strategies now that you used in Accumulation Land, your portfolio could suffer a grievous wound.

You may need a guide in this new land who can help to keep you safe. You need a financial plan and a written retirement income plan based on your goals. Some advisors may not work with their clients on setting goals and establishing a reliable income. It's time consuming, for one, and it requires skill sets for which they may not have been trained. Furthermore, some advisors are simply interested in transactions, not a nurturing relationship. They are more hunter than farmer.

Like any journey of any distance through an unknown area, without a guide and without a clear picture of your finances, it would seem to be difficult to know for certain whether you will make it to your destination. You may be overly confident and outlast your money. Or you may live in fear, frugal to a fault, when a guide could reassure you that you have money aplenty. How sad to forsake a chance to make the memory of a lifetime, all because you fretted that it would cost too much.

This is how my team and I help our clients: We strive to figure out how and when they can afford to retire. We establish plans designed to help them not outlive their money. We help them clearly understand their financial picture in an uncertain world. We help family businesses with an exit strategy. We work to help clients get back on track financially after real estate and stock market losses. Our goal is to help them simplify their financial life, paying attention to details, and working to help them build a lasting legacy for their family and causes they support the most.

We focus on big picture solutions for big picture problems. In my opinion, you may be better served with an array of experienced help, and as your primary advisor I can coordinate that for you in what we call "The Advisor Alliance." We call in people of unique ability to take a look at your specific concerns. I work with a number of tax professionals, for example; some specialize in helping families and some with helping small businesses. We can get you help, if necessary, from estate planning attorneys, divorce attorneys, business attorneys, and more. I match their abilities with your needs, and their personalities with yours. It's crucial that we all get along.

I believe strongly that you have to know what you don't know. It's good to sit down for a cup of coffee and a second opinion. I also believe that often it's not what you don't know that hurts you, but rather it's what you think to be absolutely true—but that isn't—that hurts you. I hope that in this book I have shared some valuable knowledge and exploded some dangerous myths.

I wish you well in Distribution Land—and now that you know where you are going and are well-equipped for your travels, that your sojourn will be not only safe but joyous under a pleasant sun.

{ APPENDIX }

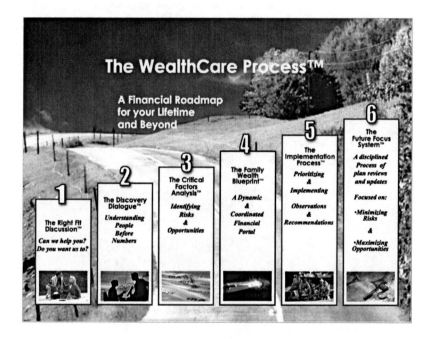

Timing Is Everything

You may be living more years in retirement than previous generations, so your investments need to last longer than ever. To demonstrate how market fluctuations may impact your portfolio when you begin to take income, let's look at two hypothetical portfolios with the same initial $200,000 investment amount and a

Positive Initial Returns Can Provide More Income

Because markets were up during the early years, Investor A was able to take annual withdrawals for more than 20 years—despite a market decline in the last half of that time period. Investor A's contract value was also three times the original investment.

It's Difficult to Recover from Early Losses

The early losses for Investor B created a situation from which it is difficult to recover. Investor B took withdrawals from a smaller pool of funds and completely depleted his or her assets in 19 years.

S&P 500® index 1989–2008. Past performance does not guarantee future results.

The results shown are intended to demonstrate the impact of

20-year period (1989–2008) of the S&P 500® index with an average rate of return of 10.36%. The difference is that Investor A experiences market declines in the last half of a 20-year period and Investor B has a market decline immediately after retiring and in three of the next eight years.

The Need for Protection

After taking income for 20 years, Investor A still had funds left. Without a plan to protect assets or a guaranteed income stream, Investor B ran out of money almost two years before the end of the 20-year period.

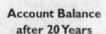

Account Balance after 20 Years

Retirement planning doesn't end with your last paycheck; circumstances may require you to take additional steps to protect your assets to ensure your long-term comfort.

Discover how you can help protect your retirement income with an annuity.

the effect of market performance on retirement assets, assuming 5% annual withdrawals of $10,000 (increasing at 3% annually for inflation). If fees and charges had been included, investment results would have been lower.

The Sequence of Returns

You can see from these charts how even a single down year at the beginning of a long period can have a devastating effect on the value of assets a client

			Investor A—Early Gain		
Year	Rate of Return	Balance after Returns	Withdrawal % of Initial Investment	Amount Withdrawn	End-of-Year Balance
1	31.69%	$263,380	5%	$10,000	$253,380
2	–3.10%	$245,525	5.15%	$10,300	$235,225
3	30.47%	$306,898	5.30%	$10,609	$296,289
4	7.62%	$318,867	5.46%	$10,927	$307,939
5	10.08%	$338,980	5.63%	$11,255	$327,725
6	1.32%	$332,050	5.80%	$11,593	$320,458
7	37.58%	$440,886	5.97%	$11,941	$428,945
8	22.96%	$527,431	6.15%	$12,299	$515,132
9	33.36%	$686,980	6.33%	$12,668	$674,313
10	28.58%	$867,031	6.52%	$13,048	$853,984
11	21.04%	$1,033,662	6.72%	$13,439	$1,020,223
12	–9.10%	$927,382	6.92%	$13,842	$913,540
13	–11.89%	$804,920	7.13%	$14,258	$790,663
14	–22.10%	$615,926	7.34%	$14,685	$601,241
15	28.68%	$773,677	7.56%	$15,126	$758,551
16	10.88%	$841,081	7.79%	$15,580	$825,501
17	4.91%	$866,033	8.02%	$16,047	$849,986
18	15.79%	$984,199	8.26%	$16,528	$967,671
19	5.49%	$1,020,796	8.51%	$17,024	$1,003,772
20	–37.00%	$632,376	8.77%	$17,535	$614,841
Totals				$268,704 +	$614,841

10.36% Average Rate of Return   **Total Benefit = $883,545**

Guarantees, including optional benefits, are subject to Pacific Life's claims-paying ability and do not protect the value of the variable investment options, which are subject to market risk. The value of the variable investment options will fluctuate and, when redeemed, may be worth more or less than the original cost. Annuity withdrawals and other distributions of taxable amounts, including death

may have. The chart for Investor B shows the returns inverted as compared to Investor A.

	Investor B—Early Loss				
Year	Rate of Return	Balance after Returns	Withdrawal % of Initial Investment	Amount Withdrawn	End-of-Year Balance
1	-37.00%	$126,000	5%	$10,000	$116,000
2	5.49%	$122,368	5.15%	$10,300	$112,068
3	15.79%	$129,764	5.30%	$10,609	$119,155
4	4.91%	$125,006	5.46%	$10,927	$114,078
5	10.88%	$126,492	5.63%	$11,255	$115,237
6	28.68%	$148,292	5.80%	$11,593	$136,700
7	-22.10%	$106,488	5.97%	$11,941	$94,548
8	-11.89%	$83,310	6.15%	$12,299	$71,011
9	-9.10%	$64,549	6.33%	$12,668	$51,882
10	21.04%	$62,798	6.52%	$13,048	$49,751
11	28.58%	$63,969	6.72%	$13,439	$50,529
12	33.36%	$67,388	6.92%	$13,842	$53,545
13	22.96%	$65,839	7.13%	$14,258	$51,582
14	37.58%	$70,965	7.34%	$14,685	$56,280
15	1.32%	$57,023	7.56%	$15,126	$41,897
16	10.08%	$46,120	7.79%	$15,580	$30,540
17	7.62%	$32,867	8.02%	$16,047	$16,820
18	30.47%	$21,944	8.26%	$16,528	$5,416
19	-3.10%	$5,248	8.51%	$5,248	$0
20	31.69%				$0
Totals				$239,392 +	$0

10.36% Average Rate of Return   Total Benefit = $239,392

benefit payouts, will be subject to ordinary income tax. For nonqualified contracts, an additional 3.8% tax may apply on net investment income beginning in 2013. If withdrawals and other distributions are taken prior to age 59½, an additional 10% federal tax may apply. Withdrawals may reduce the value of the death benefit and any optional benefits.

This material is not intended to be used, nor can it be used by any taxpayer, for the purpose of avoiding U.S. federal, state, or local tax penalties. This material is written to support the promotion or marketing of the transaction(s) or matter(s) addressed by this material. Pacific Life, its distributors, and respective representatives do not provide tax, accounting, or legal advice. Any taxpayer should seek advice based on the taxpayer's particular circumstances from an independent tax advisor or attorney.

You should carefully consider a variable annuity's risks, charges, limitations, and expenses, as well as the risks, charges, expenses, and investment goals of the underlying investment options. This and other information about Pacific Life are provided in the product and the underlying fund prospectuses. These prospectuses are available from your financial advisor or by calling the toll-free numbers listed below. Read them carefully before investing.

IRAs and qualified plans—such as 401(k)s and 403(b)s—are already tax-deferred. Therefore, a deferred annuity should be used only to fund an IRA or qualified plan to benefit from the annuity's features other than tax deferral. These include lifetime income, death benefit options, and the ability to transfer among investment options without sales or withdrawal charges.

Pacific Life refers to Pacific Life Insurance Company and its affiliates, including Pacific Life & Annuity Company. Insurance products are issued by Pacific Life Insurance Company in all states except New York and in New York by Pacific Life & Annuity Company. Product availability and features may vary by state. Each insurance company is solely responsible for the financial obligations accruing under the products it issues. Insurance product and rider guarantees, including optional benefits and any fixed subaccount crediting rates or annuity payout rates, are backed by the financial strength and claims-paying ability of the issuing insurance company and do not protect the value of the variable investment options. They are not backed by the broker/dealer from which this annuity is purchased, by the insurance agency from which this annuity is purchased, or any affiliates of those entities and none makes any representations or guarantees regarding the claims-paying ability of the issuing insurance company.

Variable insurance products are distributed by **Pacific Select Distributors, Inc.** (member FINRA & SIPC), a subsidiary of Pacific Life Insurance Company and an affiliate of Pacific Life & Annuity Company (Newport Beach, CA), and are available through licensed third-party broker/dealers

{ INDEX }

A

Accredited 9,10

Advisor 10-12, 27, 30-31, 35-36, 42,
46, 50, 53, 56-66, 69-80, 87,
93-93, 98, 105, 111, 114-118,
125-126, 131,141,154-156,
168-169, 176

Annuities 82-83, 99, 101, 104,111,
124, 140-141, 164

    Fixed 83, 99, 101-102, 111

    Insurance protection 133

    Premiums 140, 153

    Surrender charges 140

    Variable annuities 104

Asset allocation 65, 82-83, 88-89

    cash flow needs 101

Assets 20, 34, 50, 57-59, 63, 70, 73,
75, 79-80, 83, 91, 94, 96-97,
106, 108, 113, 117, 119, 131,
134-137, 159-167

    liquid 83, 94-96, 99-102, 123,
162

Auto insurance 69

B

Baby boom 44, 108

Bear markets 78, 85, 89, 93

Bonds 39-40, 79-81, 89, 95, 99, 105,
121-122, 125

    Corporate 95

    Interest rates and process 26,
80-81, 121-122

    Municipal 124-125

C

Cash flow 32, 44, 89, 101-102, 112

CDs 25-26, 39-40, 80, 105, 111,
120-121, 124-125, 132, 135, 139

Charitable 113, 157, 163-165

College education expenses 57

D

Death benefit 139-140, 152, 162-163,
176

Disclosure information 71

Diversification 80, 89, 99

Dividends 124

Dollar-cost averaging 87-88, 98, 110

Dreams and goals 16, 53, 57, 62,
88-89, 93, 167

E

Economics 167

    Health care 26, 28, 38, 131

Pensions 17, 46, 83, 143-144, 146

Social Security 28, 42, 44, 46, 92-94, 96-97, 105-108, 110, 114, 124-125

Estate planning 67, 126, 166, 169

Exchange-traded funds (ETFs) 82, 111

Expenses 29, 32, 93, 96-97, 113, 125, 130, 176

Income requirements 110

F

Financial advisors 10, 20, 31, 42, 131

Fixed annuities 111

G

Goals 33-35, 43, 52-58, 61, 72, 75, 70, 84, 91-92, 105, 108-109, 113, 155-157, 167-168, 176

Greed 27

H

Health care 26, 29, 38, 131

Health insurance 134

I

Income 10, 17-20, 25-29, 32-35, 37, 39, 42-44, 47-51, 54-55, 62-66, 80, 82-85, 87-88, 90-104, 107-111, 117, 120, 122-125, 129, 132, 134, 136, 138, 140-141, 143-145, 147, 153-154, 158, 164, 168, 176

Inflation 19, 26, 29, 36, 38, 40, 48, 79, 82-84, 87, 89, 93-96, 101-102, 108, 116-122, 131-132, 139, 156-157

Insurance 9, 11-12, 37, 45, 59, 63-64, 66, 69, 73, 81-82, 92, 94-95, 105, 113, 126, 129-135, 137-141, 152-153, 158, 162-163, 176-177

Interest rates 26, 80-81, 105, 121-122

Investments 26

Investors 49, 54, 63, 75, 78-79, 85, 104, 122, 124, 143-144

Accredited 9, 10

Accumulation phase 118

IRS - 125, 143, 146, 148-149

L

Legacy planning 165-166

Legal issues

Estate planning 67, 126, 166, 169

Lawsuits 161

Life insurance 11, 45, 59, 69, 82, 92, 105, 129, 139-140, 152-153, 158-159, 162-163, 176-177

Long-term care insurance 37, 132, 134-135,

M

Medicare 133-134

Models and formulas

Asset allocation 65, 82-83, 88-89

Municipal bonds 125

Mutual funds 63, 69, 82, 105

O

OPM 141

P

Pension plans 94

Portfolio 26, 28, 35, 39, 69, 75, 78-85,
88-89, 94, 98-103, 110-112,
116-118, 122, 149, 168

Probate 117, 126-127, 160-161

R

Retirement 10, 25-35, 39, 41-46, 48-58,
62-67, 78, 82-84, 87-101, 104-110,
113-115, 117-119, 124, 127,
129-131, 143-149, 158, 168

Risk 27, 36, 40, 42, 45, 48, 64, 71,
78-79, 85, 87, 89, 95-96, 98, 100,
103, 105, 109-111, 116-118, 121,
130, 143, 149

Roth IRA 148

S

Savings 19, 36-37, 42, 45, 48, 56, 78,
93, 95, 97, 114, 122, 124, 131, 143,
146, 157-158, 167

Stock market 19, 48-49, 64, 83, 144,
169

Stocks 26, 79-81, 89, 92, 95, 99, 105,
121-122

T

Taxes 29, 36, 38, 48, 75, 96, 113,
122-125, 140, 146-148, 152-154,
158-159, 161

V

Variable annuities 104

Veterans 138

W

Wall street 45, 88-89

CPSIA information can be obtained at www.ICGtesting.com
Printed in the USA
BVOW03s1741311014

373174BV00002B/2/P